POSITIVE CHANGE

POSITIVE CHANGE

Programming Yourself for a Change You Desire

Onaolapo Gabriel Olusola

PARTRIDGE
A Penguin Random House Company

Print information available on the last page.

To order additional copies of this book, contact
Toll Free 0800 990 914 (South Africa)
+44 20 3014 3997 (outside South Africa)
orders.africa@partridgepublishing.com

www.partridgepublishing.com/africa

CONTENTS

This book is dedicated to my number-one prayer warrior and confidant, who wrestled on behalf of our family until our story changed positively—my mother, *Madam Onaolapo Lydia Monisola.*

PREFACE

I am excited for you! I see a new day, a new dawn ahead. Something good and positive is about to happen in your life. A new chapter for your life, home, business, career, and children is about to be opened. I see an end to the same old, negative, and damning story of your life. You have been selected to be a recipient of unusual divine visitation that will lift you up from the pit of misery, tears, and failure and catapult you to an enviable height where you will be celebrated.

God is ever and always ready to change your story, but you must position yourself not to miss His moves, and your cooperation to translate this to a reality cannot be overemphasized. The Bible is full of real people with real stories. Even today, we read of real people whose stories are exciting and inspiring. You can be listed among them.

Have a glance through His lists.

- Sarah: from barrenness to fruitfulness
- Moses: from being a fugitive to being a leader of Israel
- Saul: from obscurity to kingship and stardom
- Jabesh: from failure to astonishing success
- Obed-Edom: from lack to abundance within three months

- Esther: from a slave girl to a queen of Medo-Persia
- Job: from severe losses to double restoration
- Joseph: from prison to palace
- Mary: from a humble, unknown background to a globally and eternally celebrated mother
- Saul of Tarsus: from being a terrorist to a global preacher.

And there are countless hosts of others too numerous to mention. God is the same yesterday, today, and forever!

Dear reader, I don't know what your story is at the moment or what you are passing through, but I have a feeling, a positive one, that your story is about to change. A new, good, and great story is about to be written about your finances, your marriage, your health, your errant child, your business, your ministry, your political aspiration, and your spiritual life.

Packaged into this small book are time-tested principles and teachings that will help you and guide you in your quest for a change of story and break the shackles of the evil status quo that have plagued your generation for a long time. Through an encounter with this book, your life, work, business, career, and finances cannot remain the same.

Welcome on board as you join the train and throng of people whose destinies and stories are about to be changed.

Bon voyage!

Onaolapo Gabriel Olusola
Apostle of freedom
August 2015
Lagos, Nigeria

ACKNOWLEDGEMENT

I owe deep gratitude to a number of people for the success of this book project.

To our wonderful staff of VOREP; Ademisoye Olufunke (business manager), Babalola Rachael, and others, I say thank you. A special mention should be made of Madam Adeoye Taiwo and Ademisoye Adegbenga for their support in getting this book published.

Mention should all be made of the entire members of Christ the King Rescue Global Ministry for their unwavering love and dogged dedication to our fast-growing ministry and for their unparalleled support emotionally, materially, mentally, and financially.

I will not also forget the wonderful people in Partridge Africa Inc., especially Geraldine Samson (a senior publishing consultant), Marie Giles and Rebecca Carter (publishing services associate) for their encouragement and support to make this project a huge success.

Last but not the least are the members of my immediate family—my dear wife, Florence Adenike Taiwo Onaolapo, and our children, Winner Onaolapo, Miracle Onaolapo, Freedom Onaolapo, and Queen Onaolapo. Thanks for your support.

NOTE TO THE READER

No condition is permanent. You are a complex and wonderful creation from the Almighty God. Your mind is so vast that it can absorb anything.

Unknowingly, there are things you have picked up along the line in your journey that seems to be stopping you from achieving your lofty goals. This is so terrible that you feel stuck and helpless sometimes. But this supposes not to be so. You can change anything or any situation you don't like into what you like.

There is in you enormous power to do it. You can deprogramme your mind and delete all those negative beliefs that are inimical to your success in life or reprogramme your mind with success-provoking principles that will guarantee the positive change you so much desire. Your fate and conditions are not cast in iron. Change—a good, notable, life-enhancing change—is a possibility.

I bring unto you through this book a set of keys that will be helpful to you in your quest for a positive change that will enable you to live the life you have long been dreaming of. Luckily enough, these keys are readily accessible to you, and you are the only person who can choose not to use them, thereby confining your existence to mockery, failure, pain, and opprobrium that will lead to miserable living without meaningful impacts.

The decision is completely yours to either use these keys or not.

The strength of this small book is that it is packaged in such a way that you can choose to read it beginning from any point or chapter as each chapter is independent of others, though reading them all will provide you a better chance, standing, and power to be who you choose to become in life irrespective of your present situation.

The key principles penned down in this book are time tested and failure-proof since they are derived and grounded in the Bible, the bestselling book of all time, which enjoys divine backing through the inspiration-filled revelations spanning several hundreds of years.

I enjoin you to find a place to relax with a marker in your hand to highlight any point, line, paragraph, or passage that will appeal to and address your situation for easy future reference.

Welcome to the edge of a lane that leads you to the better and brighter future you have desired for the past years. This is your time, and it's your turn to experience a positive, marvellous, and glorious change.

CHAPTER 1

THE POWER OF DIRECTION IN A CHANGE OF STORY

The Lord had said to Abram 'leave your country, your people and your father's household and go to the land I will show you. I will make you into a great nation and I will bless you; I will make your name great, and you will be a blessing. I will bless those who bless you and whoever curses you I will curse; and all peoples on earth will be blessed through you.' So Abraham left, as the Lord had told him; and Lot went with him. Abram was seventy-five years old and he set out from Haran. He took his wife Sarai, his nephew Lot, all the possessions they had accumulated and the people they had acquired in Haran, and they set out for the land of Canaan, and they arrived there.

Genesis 12:1–5

Your success or failure in life will be largely predicated on the direction you have received or not received. If you want to have accelerated progress and destiny fulfilment, right direction is equally needed. Many today have jaundiced and retarded destinies because they got it wrong in the areas of the course of study, the vocation to take up, the spouse to marry, the place to live in, whether to remain in their countries of nativity or to relocate to foreign lands. Getting it right in the areas enumerated above has helped many people to achieve success and unimaginable greatness in life. If you don't want to be a failure and end up frustrated, a great premium must be placed on getting direction and getting it early enough or at the right time.

The passage quoted above gives us the story of one who would have ended up being a great failure in life but eventually became the greatest and the most favoured human being as far as the world history reveals. This is Father Abraham. And the simple reason for his phenomenal success and greatness was due to the direction he received at the age of 75. He was instructed to leave his country, leave his people and his father's household and move to a strange land he had never been to. His obedience to this simple direction from God brought about his greatness. Three leading religions in the world can be traced to Abraham—Judaism, Christianity, and Islam. His offspring, both biological and spiritual, are in control of the world today.

Earlier on, I claimed that he was the greatest human that ever lived because he was the progenitor of people like Isaac, Jacob, Esau, Ishmael, the Arabs, King David, King Solomon, the Midianites, and the Jews, which populate the world today. Of course, he was the ancestor of Jesus Christ, the Saviour of the world. All these would not have been possible but for the direction he got.

Nothing can be as frustrating as to when you don't know what to do and where to go. A man that does not have direction is no different from an animal that roams the street aimlessly.

A. WHAT IS DIRECTION?

Direction is having instructions on what to do and how to do it with step-by-step guidelines.

1. Direction means taking the right step at the right time.
2. Direction is going to the right place or right person at the right time.
3. Direction is saying the right thing at the right time.

Direction is a factor that gave me an edge in the ministry. In the year 1994, I was at a crossroads in taking up a pastoral job. I had three offers—two in Lagos (commercial capital of Nigeria) and one in Abuja (political capital). After I prayed, the Lord did not only direct me to go to Lagos but chose one of the two mission stations for me. The one the Lord chose was full of challenges because of the crises I met when I resumed my pastoral assignment there and without a pastorium. I had to sleep under the table in the senior pastor's office until I became frustrated and left to take Abuja's pastoral offer against the Lord's directive. After about two months, the Lord instructed me through a prophet, the late M. O. Titilayo, that He the Lord did not send me to Abuja and that I should go back to the former mission station, so I reluctantly obeyed.

This obedience became more difficult considering the differences in the two places. The Lagos mission post offered me a monthly salary of 1,470 naira without an accommodation, while the Abuja mission offered me a monthly salary of 9,000 naira and a two-bedroom flat.

However, I continued my ministry there for over seven years. The Lord greatly blessed me. I got married, bore twins, had my own car, published my first book, and even had a land property, not to mention some destiny-promoting people that I met in Lagos that are too numerous to mention.

Within these same years, I was receiving information about the developments in the Abuja mission post, which I had run to initially. The senior pastor there died mysteriously after vomiting blood, and the associate pastor that replaced me also died after mysteriously vomiting blood, but today I am alive with a flourishing ministry in Lagos.

B. WAYS TO GET DIRECTION

1. By studying the Word of God: When last did you read/study the *Word*? You need to dig deep into His Word. And that was why the psalmist said:

   Your word is a lamp to my feet
   And a light for my path. (Psalm 119:105)

2. Through meditative prayer: Not just any prayer, but it has to be a meditative prayer. Prayer is a two-way communication. When you talk to God, He will talk to you in return.

3. Through dreams: Dreams are important ways that the Lord uses in directing His children. But please note that not everybody has the gift of dreams.

Even some of those that have the gift neglect it. God never neglects anybody. He speaks to everybody.

> For God does speak—now one way, now another—though man may not perceive it. In a dream, in a vision of the night, when deep sleep falls on men as they slumber in their beds. (Job 33:14–15)

4. Through vision: This is similar to dreams. Not everybody is gifted in this area too.
5. Through third parties: A third party could be your pastor, prophet, parents, counsellor, and even your children. Never neglect the advice of people.

C. POWERS OF DIRECTION

1. It gives you an edge over competitors or enemies. David got an edge over his enemies by enquiring from the Lord in 2 Samuel 5:18–19.
2. It gives you profit on your endeavour.

> This is what the Lord says—your Redeemer, the Holy one of Israel: I am the Lord your God, who teaches you what is best for you, who directs you in the way you should go. (Isaiah 48–17)

3. It commands speed in your journey to greatness. David also enquired from the Lord on where to go, and the Lord gave directions, as seen in 2 Samuel 2:1. David succeeded because he sought direction from God.

4. It distinguishes you from ordinary animals.

> I will instruct you and teach you in the way you
> should go; I will counsel you and watch over you.
> Do not be like the horse or the mule, which have
> no understanding but must be controlled by bit
> and bridle or they will not come to you. (Psalm
> 32:8, 9)

5. It makes you a mysterious being. When you are operating by direction, it will be difficult for people to understand or even predict your next move.

6. It brings about a change of story. Father Abraham's story and my humble self's story are enough proof that direction brings about change of story. Because Father Abraham took the directive from God, he had a change of story. I pray that you will have such encounter as you begin to listen and obey divine directives in Jesus' name.

7. It guarantees a stress-free race.

> I will guide you in the way of wisdom and lead
> you along straight paths. When you walk, your
> steps will not be hampered; when you run, you
> will not stumble. (Proverbs 4:11–12)

8. It makes your assignment easy and successful.

> During the night Paul had a vision of a man of
> Macedonia standing and begging him, 'Come
> over to Macedonia.' (Acts 16:9)

Note: This was the beginning of the evangelization of Europe, which led to global evangelization, with the attendant spread of civilization, education, human rights, and economic prosperity.

Acts 16:6 says, 'Having been kept by the Holy Spirit from preaching the word in the province of Asia.' This verse has been troubling my mind for several years now.

Why did the Holy Spirit forbid the preaching of the gospel to Asians first but rather chose Europe?

I have conjectured two to three reasons. But since this isn't a polemic or an apologetic work and neither is it a research-based one, I leave the reader to ponder and find answer(s) to it.

Time spent in seeking direction is never wasted time. Seek direction and pray for direction if you want your story to change. Henceforth, you will never lack direction in your life in Jesus' precious name!

CHAPTER 2

POSITIONING YOURSELF FOR A CHANGE OF STORY

Then the king ordered Ashpenaz, chief of his court officials, to bring into the king's service some of the Israelites from the royal family and the nobility—young men without any physical defect, handsome, showing aptitude for every kind of learning, well informed, quick to understand, and qualified to serve in the king's palace. He was to teach them the language and literature of the Babylonians. The king assigned them a daily amount of food and wine from the king's table. They were to be trained for three years, and after that they were to enter the king's service. Among those who were chosen were some from Judah: Daniel, Hananiah, Mishael and Azariah. The chief official gave them new names: to Daniel, the name Belteshazzar; to Hananiah, Shadrach; to Mishael Meshach; and to Azariah, Abednego. . . . To these four young men God gave knowledge and understanding of all kinds of literature and learning. And Daniel could understand visions and dreams of all kinds.

At the end of the time set by the king to bring them into his service, the chief official presented them to Nebuchadnezzar. The king talked with them, and he found none equal to Daniel, Hananiah, Mishael and Azariah; so they entered the king's service. In every matter of wisdom and understanding about which the king questioned them, he found them ten times better than all the magicians and enchanters in his whole kingdom. And Daniel remained there until the first year of King Cyrus.

Daniel 1:3–21

It has been said that one is lucky only when adequate preparation meets with opportunity. Opportunity is also said to be a haughty goddess who waits for no one and that to not miss an opportunity whenever it shows up, preparation must be in place to embrace it. My intention is to help you in positioning yourself for a change of story, to challenge you to prepare mentally, spiritually, vocationally, professionally, and even financially to seize the opportunity that may come your way in the near or far future.

Note: to serve in the palace, you must be prepared and qualified!

The quotation above gives details about the story of Daniel and his three friends—Hananiah, Mishael, and Azariah (popularly known as Shadrach, Meshach and Abednego, the names given to them by their Babylonian lords). These four people were not the only captives taken from Jerusalem to Babylon and neither were they the only captives recruited to serve in the government of Babylon.

But right from day one of their recruitment, they decided to be different and to make a difference. They distinguished themselves through consecration, diligence, attention to details, finesse, and excellent delivery of whatever assignment they were given. The Bible says they were found ten times better than all the magicians and astrologers in the realm. This is the positioning we are talking about, not lobbying for favour or position one is not qualified for.

I want to challenge you, my reader, to from this moment make continuous efforts to upgrade yourself in the area of your calling or career. Engage in self-development exercise, read books, attend seminars and conferences, befriend serious-minded people, go to school for further studies if need be, hone your skills, don't be satisfied with mediocrity and average performance, and change your associates and companions if it will help in the course of positioning yourself.

Another area of self-positioning for a change of story is character development. Work on your character—be loyal, dependable, trustworthy and be someone that can be vouched for. Don't be a scoundrel!

A story of someone very close to me readily comes to mind. There was a problem at his place of work due to economic downturn or recession; staffers were resigning in droves, which threatened the survival of the organization. He conferred with me and was encouraged to stay put. For close to two years, he received no pay, and the situation is better imagined than experienced, with him being a married man with children. But God eventually rewarded his loyalty to his company and boss. When the fortune of the company rejuvenated, he was placed in a rare office, where he made good money without stealing. Today, he has more than two houses in Lagos, has cars to himself, and now runs his own company.

It takes humility and readiness to come down from someone's horse to be able to position oneself sometimes.

The story of a man known as Zacchaeus in the Bible drives home this point. He was a rich man by all standards, but he needed something that money could not buy. Consequently, he decided to do the unthinkable to get what he wanted.

> Jesus entered Jericho and was passing through. A man was there by the name of Zacchaeus; he was a chief tax collector and was wealthy. He wanted to see who Jesus was, but being a short man he could not, because of the crowd. So he ran ahead and climbed a sycamore-fig tree to see him, since Jesus was coming that way.
>
> When Jesus reached the spot, he looked up and said to him, 'Zacchaeus, come down immediately I must stay at your house today.' . . . Jesus said to him, 'Today salvation has come to this house, because this man, too, is a son of Abraham.
>
> For the son of man came to seek and to save what was lost. While they were listening to this, he went on to tell them a parable, because he was near Jerusalem and the people thought that the kingdom of God was going to appear at once. (Luke 19:1–11)

Your story may not change until you make conscious efforts and take positive steps towards it. You must do something about yourself or your situation for your story to change.

Do you know that making wrong choices is not a result of ill luck or problems? It may be a result of your inability to undo your wrong decisions.

A very good example is that of Zacchaeus, who lacked inner peace though he was rich and highly placed in the society. He had all things that money could buy, but he knew something was missing in his life, and what he did not have was the greatest gift to mankind—Jesus.

The Bible describes Zacchaeus as a short man, but when he took the decision to change the story of his life by seeing Jesus, the Bible records that he ran and climbed a tree. He did not allow his height to deny him the opportunity of seeing Jesus. Zacchaeus knew that one was empty without Jesus, and he also knew that Jesus would not intrude until he positioned himself, so he did.

Similarly, the prodigal son made the wrong choice, but he also made a U-turn when he realized he was on the wrong path. Remember, there is a saying that man is the architect of his fortune or misfortune. The prodigal son determined to position himself for a change of story. He made a mistake by asking his father for his inheritance prematurely. He lavishly spent it all, and he ended up working as a labourer, feeding pigs—despite the fact that Israelites detest pigs. But the Bible tells us that he woke up one day and decided to make a U-turn by going back to beg his father for forgiveness. His story did not end there; his father not only took him back, but he also celebrated him.

> When he came to his senses, he said, 'How many of my father's hired servants have food to spare, and here I am starving to death! I will set out and go back to my father and say to him: Father, I have

sinned against heaven and against you. I am no longer worthy to be called your son; make me like one of your hired servants.' So he got up and went to his father. . . . 'For this son of mine was dead and is alive again; he was lost and is found.' So they began to celebrate. (Luke 15:17–24)

Beloved, it is high time you had a rethink and take steps that can change the story of your life. May the good Lord guide you as you do so. Amen!

WAYS TO POSITION YOURSELF

1. Mentally

You can position yourself mentally by furthering your education, attending seminars and workshops, and reading books. Leaders are readers, and there is a saying that leaders are not born but are made. Indeed, every reader is a potential leader.

Bishop David Oyedepo said that 'information is the mother of manifestation' and that 'if you are not informed, you will be deformed'.

Chief Jeremiah Awolowo also said that the day you stop learning, you start to decay. Wait a minute! Since you graduated from school, how many books have you read? Remember that learning is a continuous exercise. Myles Munroe describes reading as 'two brains having intercourse'.

2. Spiritually

It is high time you tuned to the frequency of God. Mend the broken fences with Him. Go back to the altar of prayer and holiness; make the Bible your pocketbook and best companion by studying the Word.

> Do not let this book of the law depart from your mouth; meditate on it day and night, so that you may be careful to do everything written in it. Then you will be prosperous and successful. (Joshua 1:8)

I know and am very sure that no man can have good success without being spiritually sound.

3. Physically

Learn how to relate with people. Mend your broken relationships and discover new friends. There are three dimensions of relationships, namely:

(i)   relationship with God
(ii) relationship with people
(iii) relationship with yourself.

Be well mannered and polite to people. Be kind to others and encourage them. Show love to everybody at all times.

4. Financially

Be wise. Consult financial experts if there is any need for it. Shun your pride and arrogance. Be investment savvy and don't be a prodigal.

STEPS TO TAKE FOR EFFECTIVE POSITIONING

1. Shun Arrogance

If Zacchaeus had not shunned arrogance (but thinking of his great wealth and high position in the society), it is possible that his life would not have changed for the better. You need to humble yourself. Naaman also shunned arrogance, and he was healed of leprosy.

> So he went down and dipped himself in the Jordan seven times, as the man of God had told him, and his flesh was restored and clean like that of a young boy. (2 King 5:14)

The Bible says that pride goes before destruction and God beholds the proud from afar (Proverbs 16:18 and Psalm 138:6). The Holy Spirit cannot live inside anyone that is proud and full of himself.

2. Defy Obstacles

Obstacles are not hindrances, as popularly believed, but stepping stones to greatness (Luke 19:3). Be patient; don't be in a hurry in the presence of God. Be a careful planner, but don't always wait for perfect conditions.

3. Shun Shame

Somebody said that the key to the kingdom is in asking.

> Ask and it will be given to you; seek and you will find; knock and the door will be opened to you. (Matthew 7:7)

Zacchaeus ran to climb the sycamore tree, not caring about his position and financial status. Neither was he interested in what the people around him would say. You should accept that there will always be critics. Learn to stay focused.

4. Shun Opposition or Criticism

Oftentimes, all the critics want to do is to distract you. Do not pay attention to them. Zacchaeus did not care what the people around him were saying. He was focused, and he achieved his goal; he was once a sinner but is now a saint through salvation in Christ Jesus. (Luke 19:7)

I pray that God will give you the courage and the confidence that you need to position yourself for a change of story.

CHAPTER 3

THREE-DIMENSIONAL ANOINTING IN A CHANGE OF STORY

Then Samuel took a flask of olive oil, and poured it over Saul's head and kissed him, saying, 'Has not the Lord anointed you leader over his inheritance? When you leave me today, you will meet two men near Rachael's tomb, at Zelzah on the border of Benjamin. They will say to you, "The donkeys you set out to look for have been found. And now your father has stopped thinking about them and is worried about you.

He is asking, 'What shall I do about my son?'" . . . After that you will go to Gibeah of God, where there is a philistine outpost. As you approach the town, you will meet a procession of prophets coming down from the high place with lyres, tambourines, flutes and harps being played before them, and they will be prophesying. The spirit of the Lord will come upon you in power, and you will prophesy with them; and you will be changed into a different person. Once these signs are fulfilled, do whatever you find to do, for God is with you.'

(1 Samuel 10:1–7)

The story in this passage shows us how someone can step into popularity from obscurity by being anointed. Saul, a Benjamite (the smallest tribe in Israel), inadvertently had an encounter with the prophet Samuel while on a mission to search for his father's lost asses. Prior to this time, the children of Israel have been clamouring to have a monarch as their ruler because they were fed up with the leadership style of the two sons of the prophet Samuel. After the prophet Samuel's initial resistance and aversion to this request, the Lord instructed him to listen to his people and anoint for them a leader. Few days before Saul's visitation to Samuel, God had instructed Samuel of Saul's visit and that he was to be anointed as the new king. Consequent upon Saul being anointed, the Bible says, 'And the spirit of the Lord came upon Saul.' This is empowerment.

WHAT IS ANOINTING?

1. *Anointing* means 'empowerment'—empowerment in the sense that one will be able to do the impossible and things that are naturally difficult. This empowerment makes one a candidate of exploits and a mysterious being. When someone is anointed, it means he/she has the power to perform miracles, signs, and wonders, and most particularly, he/she has the presence of the Almighty God in his/her life.

2. *Anointing* means setting someone apart.

> I baptize you with water, but He will baptize you
> with the Holy Spirit! (Mark 1:8)

The reason for John's assertion (as stated in the quotation above) is that Jesus Christ was carrying the anointing, which enabled Him to baptize people with the Holy Spirit. This kind of baptism is different from water baptism, which John's ministry was restricted to.

Once you have this anointing, you will become an unquestionable head. Saul was anointed, and nobody could question his kingship. Let me add here that you won't be ordinarily set apart, but you will be set apart for special assignment. Examples of anointed people are Jesus Christ, Saul, Paul, etc.

THE THREE-DIMENSIONAL ANOINTING

Human beings are of three components—spirit, soul, and body. We relate to God and the celestial world through the spirit. We relate to the terrestrial world and our environment through the body and our physical senses, while the soul or mind serves as the coordinator between the physical and spiritual realms. We decode and encode messages through the instrumentality of the mind. Each of these three components needs empowerment; that is, you need bodily, mental, and spiritual empowerment. Achieving this is what I mean by three-dimensional anointing.

1. Anointing for Bodily Empowerment

Beloved, you need to be empowered for physical exploits. You have to be on *fire*, and whatever evil thing that touches you will become stubbles. It also gives you the grace to do physically that which you cannot do ordinarily.

> Therefore when Christ came into the world he said: sacrifice and offering you did not desire, but a body you prepared for me. (Hebrew 10:5)

Do you know that Christ did not just come into the world to give himself as the sacrificial lamb but was also anointed by God for bodily empowerment? That is, God prepared a special body for Christ because of His special assignment.

> And if the spirit of Him who raised Jesus from the dead is living in you, he who raised Christ from the dead will also give life to your mortal bodies through his spirit, who lives in you. (Romans 8:11)

Anointing can quicken a dead body, including dead brain tissue and dead organs.

> The spirit of the Lord came upon him in power so that he tore the lion apart with his bare hands as he might have torn a young goat. But he told neither his father nor his mother what he had done. (Judges 14:6)

It was certain that Samson would not have been brave enough to confront the lion and kill it had he not been empowered.

2. Anointing for Mental Empowerment

Being empowered mentally will give you the grace to do exploits. It gives you the grace to operate above your competitors in the world of commerce. A person who lacks anointing can be easily compared to a person that operates with blindness of the heart.

> The god of this age has blinded the minds of unbelievers, so that they cannot see the light of the gospel of the glory of Christ, who is the image of God. (2 Corinthians 4:4)

This is similar to what is going on at this present time. A Christian who lacks anointing can never operate in the world of commerce. But when his mind is opened, he will find it very easy to operate in the world of commerce successfully. Jesus Christ said:

> For the people of this world are more shrewd in dealing with their own kind than are the people of light. (Luke 16:8)

With anointing, it won't be so in your case.

> Then Moses said to the Israelites, 'See the Lord has chosen Bezalel son of Uri, the son of Hur, of the tribe of Judah, and he has filled him with the spirit of God, with skill, ability and knowledge in all kinds of crafts—to make artistic designs for work in gold, silver and bronze, to cut and set stones, to work in wood and to engage in all kinds of artistic.' (Exodus 35:30–32)

3. Anointing for Spiritual Empowerment

> How God anointed Jesus of Nazareth with the Holy
> Spirit and with power, and how he went around
> doing good and healing all who were under the
> devil, because God was with him. (Acts of the
> Apostles 10:38)

For you to be able to record miracles in your life, business, academics, and in your ministry, you need to be empowered spiritually. Your spirit man must be alert against any form of attack. Being empowered spiritually connects you to the bandwidth of heaven to download from the Internet of God.

For supernatural accomplishment, divine direction, and divine connection, you need spiritual empowerment.

WHY THE NEED FOR THIS ANOINTING?

We are living in a world of power—positive and negative, good and evil, satanic and godly, physical and spiritual. You cannot amount to someone of note in life until the issue of empowerment is addressed. We have many today who, in the quest for power, are joining occult groups, selling their souls to Satan, or going for voodoo, black magic, talismans, and some other esoteric powers. God expressly forbids this for his children because he had made provision for empowerment to whosoever desires it.

A note of *warning*: I want to counsel you not to seek for power outside God, and if you have made this mistake, I implore you to change because even though they appear good and potent, they always have repercussions for those entangled by them and their posterity. The late John D. Rice, a doctor and reverend and a popular preacher in America, said, 'All Satan's apples have worms.' This can't be truer.

> In that day their burden will be lifted from your shoulders, their yoke from your neck; the yoke will be broken because you have grown so fat. (Isaiah 10:27, NIV)

> And it shall come to pass in that day, that his burden shall be taken away from off thy shoulder, and his yoke from off thy neck, and the yoke shall be destroyed because of the anointing. (Isaiah 10:27, KJV)

Below are the reasons for anointing:

- To break the yoke of curses (family, personal, generational, legitimate or illegitimate curses)
- To break the yoke of poverty
- To break the yoke of repeated failure
- To break the yoke of stagnation
- To break the yoke of terrestrial powers
- To break the yoke of family enemies
- To break the yoke of limitation
- To break the yoke of opposition.

Unless these yokes are destroyed, it will be difficult to achieve success. Many Christians are languishing under the yokes mentioned above and more, but you can be free from them.

THREE DIFFERENT TYPES OF ANOINTING IN THE BIBLE

1. The Leper's Anointing

This is primarily the work of salvation by the Holy Spirit for conversion to God and cleansing from the filth of sin to bring about justification and right standing before God (John 3:5–6; Romans 8:9; 1 Corinthians 12:3; Romans 8:16). The focus here is *justification*.

2. The Priest's Anointing

This is the anointing to holy living, consecration to service, and godly living with emphasis on righteousness. The New Testament teaches that all believers are priests (1 Peter 2:9; Revelation 1:6; Exodus 30:1–30, Exodus 29:1–46; Leviticus 8:1). The focus here is *consecration* and *sanctification*.

3. The King's Anointing

This is the work of the Holy Spirit to confer on and release power to believers for exploits. Special grace and authority to function in an office effectively and efficiently are given. (Acts 1:4, 2:1–4, 4:23, 5:12; 1 John 2:27; Matthew 3:11). The focus here is on *empowerment*.

Therefore, as a believer, you are expected to seek and experience these three types of anointing.

HOW TO RECEIVE ANOINTING

1. You need to consecrate yourself. This means setting one's self apart, denying the flesh of pleasure and staying away from sins.

> Peter replied, 'Repent and be baptized, every one of you, in the name of Jesus Christ for the forgiveness of your sins. And you will receive the gift of the Holy Spirit.' (Acts 2:38)

2. You must thirst for it. This means having a strong desire for anointing, like someone who is thirsty for water on a sunny day.

> On the last and greatest day of the feast, Jesus stood and said in a loud voice, 'If anyone is thirsty, let him come to me and drink. Whoever believes in me, as the scriptures has said, streams of living water will flow from within him, 'By this he meant the spirit, whom those who believed in him were later to receive. Up to that time the Spirit had not been given, since Jesus had not yet been glorified.' (John 7:37–39)

3. Set time apart for fasting and prayer. Anointing doesn't come by mere wishing. You need to seek the face of God through fasting and prayers—long sessions of prayers if need be until you receive it.

> Then Jesus was led by the spirit into the desert to be tempted by the devil. After fasting forty days and forty nights, he was hungry. (Matthew 4:1–11)

4. Learn to use the power of praise. Praise cannot be underestimated in your quest for the anointing. Praise moves God to release His grace and power.

> It is good to praise the LORD and make music to your name, O most high, to proclaim your love in the morning and your faithfulness at night.
> You have exalted my horn like that of a wild ox; fine oils have been poured upon me. (Psalm 92:1, 2, 10)

5. Eat and digest the Word of God. In seeking for the anointing, let the Word of God be your companion. Read it. Study it. Meditate on it, and digest it.

> While Peter was still speaking these words, the Holy Spirit came on all who heard the message. (Acts 10:44)

> The spirit gives life; the flesh counts for nothing. The words I have spoken to you are spirit and they are life. (John 6:63)

6. Importunity—this is persistency and refusal to give up asking for anointing. God honours and encourages importunity in prayers.

> If you then, though you are evil, know how to give good gifts to your children, how much more will your Father in heaven give the Holy Spirit to those who ask him! (Luke 11:13)

Until now you have not asked for anything in my name. Ask and you will receive, and your joy will be complete. (John 16:24)

EXPLOITS OF ANOINTING

And such as do wickedly against the covenant shall he corrupt by flatteries: but the people that do know their God shall be strong, and do exploits. (Daniel 11:32)

Here I want to make a list of the few people who made exploits through the anointing.

1. Samson, who tore a lion to pieces and killed his enemies in thousands (Judges 14:1–10)
2. The prophet Elijah, who confronted and defeated godless kings and prophets of his time (1 Kings 18:16–end; 2 Kings 1:1–19)
3. The prophet Elisha, who received double portion of Prophet Elijah's power, which is evident in biblical records—while seven miracles were recorded for Elijah, fourteen were recorded for Elisha (2 Kings 13:14–20)
4. The man of God from Judah (1 Kings 13:1–10)
5. Daniel, a prophet, a politician, an astute administrator (Daniel 5:10–31; 6:1–28)
6. The apostle Paul (Acts 19:1–16)
7. The apostle Peter (Acts 9:32–42)
8. Philip the evangelist (Acts 8:26–40)

9. Bezalel, a renowned artist and designer (Exodus 35:30–33)
10. Oholiab, a great teacher and has the ability to teach and perform other skilled works (Exodus 35:34–35)
11. Jesus Christ our Lord.

> The Spirit of the Lord is on me, because he has anointed me to preach good news to the poor. He has sent me to proclaimed freedom for the prisoners and recovery of sight for the blind, to release the oppressed, to proclaim the year of the Lord's favour. (Luke 4:18–19)

> And God anointed Jesus of Nazareth with the Holy Spirit and power, and how he went around doing good and healing all who were under the power of the evil, because God was with him. (Acts 10:38)

From the above quotations, it is evident that Jesus made exploits and changed the course of world history, which is unmatched and unparalleled till today, through the anointing.

If you want to make a difference in your world and experience a change of story, seek for anointing until you have it.

CHAPTER 4

THE PLACE OF INSIGHT IN A CHANGE OF STORY

When the water in the skin was gone, she put the boy under one of the bushes.

Then she went off and sat down nearby, about a bowshot away, for she thought 'I cannot watch the boy die.' And as she sat there nearby, she began to sob.

God heard the boy crying, and the angel of God called to Hagar from heaven and said to her, 'What is the matter, Hagar? Do not be afraid God has heard the boy crying as he lies there. Lift the boy up and take him by the hand, for I will make him into a great nation.'

Then God opened her eyes and she saw a well of water. So she went and filled the skin with water and gave the boy a drink.

God was with the boy as he grew up. He lived in the desert and became an archer. While he was living in the desert of Paran, his mother got a wife for him from Egypt.

Genesis 21:15–21

The world to an uninformed and uncultured mind isn't fair and is full of problems.

Pastoral ministry has given me a rare privilege of deciphering people's thinking patterns and also of their perspectives about the world in general. I estimated that I interact with at least a thousand people yearly through my counselling ministry. I want to submit that few people—very infinitesimal—are different when it comes to the issue of insight. Larger percentages of people only see problems and talk about problems all the time—a shrinking economy, a dilapidated infrastructure, bad school curriculum, incompetent political leaders, unreliable friends, scarcity and inflation, and so many other social ills. They never seem to see good things around them. Opportunities to advance their careers, to use the potentials deposited in them, to make money by solving problems through ingenuity, and to leave a legacy by creating an invention have no meaning to this set of people.

I AM OF A DIFFERENT BREED

By His grace, I have trained myself and been helped by the Holy Spirit to always see the bright side of life no matter what the situation is. I am an optimist, and I tend to see opportunity in every situation. Someone has said, 'Every problem carries with it the seed of opportunity if only we have the eyes to see.' This is where the problem lies—having the eyes to see!

Opportunities are all around you, but the problem is that you do not see them. You remain in that situation because your eyes are not opened. The truth is that your destiny remains closed as long as your inner eyes are closed.

I want to inform you here that travelling all around cannot bring an end to your problems. Your greatest need is for your eyes to be opened.

Do you know that somebody may be working in the Central Bank of Nigeria (CBN) and still be complaining that there is no money? Many people in the midst of plenty still complain of financial problems in our country and are travelling to other countries. It is an illusion to believe that success will be found in other countries since it is a well-known fact that money is not picked on the streets of nations abroad. Your story will not change until your eyes are opened.

A former managing director who was an expatriate in a multinational company refused to leave Nigeria after he left his job. He said that he had lived in twenty-one different countries but saw Nigeria as the easiest place to make money. He was able to say this because he had acquired an insight into the workings of his host community. He saw plenty in the midst of scarcity and determined to establish a business in Nigeria, where he still lives till today.

Beloved, what you need at this juncture is not a change of business; neither do you need to travel out of the country. Oh, if only you can understand that what you need is a change of orientation. You need insight!

Pastor Matthew Ashimolowo gave a speech several years ago in which he said, 'Who you are is not a matter of where you are.' He said that a failure in Nigeria can never succeed in the United States.

In the biblical passage quoted above, Sarah pressurized her husband (Abraham) to send Hagar and her son away. She said her son (Isaac) could never live under the same roof with a slave. Maybe you are rejected by people around you as Hagar and her son were rejected, but I have good news for you. God has not given power to any man under the sun to decide your destiny in life, be it a prophet, a bishop, or even your parents.

After too much pressure, Abraham listened to the words of Sarah and sent Hagar and her son away. As she was leaving, Abraham gave her a bottle of water. Hagar left without having a destination, and the water was consumed along the way. She was perplexed and didn't know what to do. She couldn't stand to watch her only son die in her presence, so she dumped him and stayed far away from him, weeping. She did not open her eyes to look for water or possibilities around her. Many of us today also can't afford the good things in life. Could it be because we don't have money? No, the reason is that we do not see beyond the present circumstances.

Hagar threw away her only belonging. She threw away her only property. She threw away her tomorrow (Ishmael). But thank God for the divine intervention. I pray the Lord will intervene in your situation today. Amen.

God did not listen to the cry of Hagar because she was old enough to demonstrate creativity and provide for her son's needs. Brethren, what will crying do to alleviate your problem? How will sorrowing help that situation? Do not forget that Hagar and her son were unbelievers, yet God took interest in their case. God will not ignore you, dear child of God.

The angel of the Lord called Hagar, but she did not explain her predicament; she only gave excuses. At the end of the day, Sarah was the architect of Hagar's fortune or misfortunes, depending on the way you see it.

Many of us always tell ourselves that *life is not fair.* This is wrong. Hagar did not see anything good about herself. Do you know that God did not open her eyes until she took up her responsibility?

> Lift the boy up and take him by the hand. (Genesis 21:18)

If you are the type that runs away from responsibility, I am afraid that God will not open your eyes to see your riches.

The grandchildren of Hagar are controlling the world economy today in terms of petrodollars: Iraq, Iran, Libya, Saudi Arabia and the other Middle Eastern States. Their fortune is traceable to the moment God gave their ancestral grandmother, Hagar, an insight. You can also be an instrument to change the destiny of your own generation.

Beloved reader, all you need is insight. If God should open your eyes, I assure you that your story will change. The fact is that your destiny and the breakthrough that will usher you into it will remain closed until your eyes are opened.

THE POWERS OF INSIGHT

1. Insight will give you an edge over your peers: In whatever you are doing, if you have insight, being ahead of your mates become a possibility.
2. It will enable you to handle difficult situations with ease.

3. It will broaden your vision about life.
4. It will give you abundance in the midst of scarcity (Genesis 21:19).

The psalmist knew the importance of insight, and that was why he said:

> Open my eyes that I may see
> Wonderful things in your law. (Psalm 119:18)

Unless the Lord opens your eyes, you will not be able to see wonderful things around you. Great inventors and investors of note that eventually ruled their world and left indelible footprints on the sand of history are people who have unusual insight. Insight comes from the mind or heart, and this is beyond the function of the physical eyes. It is called that *wow!* moment. Archimedes called it eureka (I have found it). Archimedes was working on a particular formula, and he developed mental block until one day, while bathing, the solution came to him like a revelation. History tells us that he ran out of the bathroom, shouting, 'Eureka!' (I have found it).

I pray for insight that will transform your life in Jesus' name. Amen!

CHAPTER 5

THE PLACE OF SEED SOWING IN A CHANGE OF STORY

> Isaac planted crops in that land and the same year
> reaped a hundred fold, because the Lord blessed him.
> The man became rich and his wealth continued to
> grow until he became very wealthy. He had so many
> flocks and herds and servants that the Philistines
> envied him.
>
> Genesis 26:12–14

The passage above presents to us the story of Isaac, the son of Abraham, in the Bible. Even though he was a covenant child and in a covenant-allotted place, he experienced hardship and famine to the extent he thought of migrating from Canaan land (the Promised Land) to Egypt, which typifies the world. But by divine direction and revelation, he was forbidden from going down to Egypt and instructed to sow even though there was no rain.

His actions looked foolish to his unbelieving neighbours and attracted mockery, but right in the year of famine, the Bible made us know that he reaped a hundredfold of what he planted until he became rich, wealthy, and very wealthy, which attracted envy from the same people who made jest of him while he was sowing.

We can conveniently say Isaac discovered the irrigation method in farming, which today is helping the world to overcome seasonal drought and food shortage.

Isaac took a great risk by releasing his seed in an uncertain time, which eventually paid off. This serves as a great lesson today unto whosoever wants a change of story— sowing is always done in pains of a great risk.

If you have not learned to release what you have, you can never get answers to your prayers. If you are a stingy person, you cannot experience the goodness of the Lord.

> I tell you the truth, unless a kernel of wheat falls to the ground and dies, it remains only a single seed. But if it dies, it produces many seeds. (John 12:24)

In the passage quoted above, Jesus Christ was explaining the importance of seed-sowing to his disciples. He said that unless a seed falls to the ground, it will remain the same. In other words, Jesus Christ was figuratively speaking about His death.

God has one son, which can be referred to as a seed, but He had to leave this seed to die so as to get more seeds. And because of the seed he buried on the ground some thousands of years ago, we are now referred to as *his heirs*.

HOW DID GOD COME ABOUT HAVING MANY SONS?

God has many sons today because He gave His only son.

> For God so loved the world that He gave His one and only son that whoever believes in Him shall not perish but have eternal life. (John 3:16)

I have not heard and neither have I read of a powerful man of God who prayed on empty ridges and at the end of the day had a bountiful harvest of yams; sowing must go alongside praying. Permit me to assert that anxiety and prayer cannot bring forth miracles. You cannot become a multitude unless you die. You cannot be more than who and what you are unless you learn how to give. Prosperity cannot be invoked by prayer, but only by adherence to principles.

WHAT IS A SEED?

Let the Bible define it:

> Then God said, 'Let the land produce vegetation: seed-bearing plants and trees on the land that bear fruit and seed in it, according to their various kinds.' (Genesis 1:11)

Myles Munroe said, 'The death of a seed is the burial of a forest.'

Today, many eat their seed, which is not meant to be eaten but to be sown. If you carelessly let your seed die, you may not get the desired harvest.

There is a story about a man who sold all that he had in order to acquire land. On the eve of the day he was going to get the land, his pastor came to visit him and explained that he had an accommodation problem. The man had to sow a very painful seed by giving his pastor the whole money he had saved. And to the glory of God, today he owns more than twenty plots of land in Lagos State of Nigeria and has built three houses. He is a man I know personally, for he attends my church.

FACTS AND CHARACTERISTICS OF THE SEED

1. Every seed has the power to produce its own kind. Whenever you sow murmuring, it is very certain that you will reap murmuring. On the other hand, you will reap good works and money where you sow good works and money. It is never possible for you to plant mangoes and reap oranges. Every seed will always bring forth its own kind.

2. Seeds have the ability to multiply. Here is a practical example. If a seed of guinea corn is planted, I am very sure that after three months, over a thousand seeds will be gathered.

3. Seeds have to be sown before they can produce. If a seed is not buried, it can never produce its kind. And if you find it very difficult to believe me, why not keep a seed in the bank, and after one or two years, you can go to the bank manager and ask for your seed. It is very certain that your single seed will be given back to you. And that was why Jesus said, unless a seed is sown, it will remain like that forever.

4. Every seed needs fertile soil to flourish. If you want to sow your seed either financially or spiritually, I urge you to sow it on fertile ground.

5. Seeds have to be sown continually.

> Sow your seed in the morning, and at the evening let not your hands be idle, for you do not know which will succeed, whether this or that or whether both will do equally well. (Ecclesiastes 11:6)

You don't have to wait for a particular time before sowing seed.

> If clouds are full of water, they pour rain on earth. Whether a tree falls to the south or the north, in the place where it falls, there will it lie. Whoever watches the wind will not plant; whoever looks at the clouds will not reap. (Ecclesiastes 11:3–4)

6. Do not be too careful when it comes to sowing (Ecclesiastes 11:4). Thank God if you have been charitable and have given money to some people but it appears that you will not reap anything. Don't be discouraged, because if you decide to hold what you have, it may delay your harvest forever. No volume of prayer can change this because it is an eternal principle.

   Also, you can never be too careful because the devil can send anybody to stop you from sowing; it could be your wife, husband, or friend. So always be vigilant, and don't allow anyone to discourage you.

7. The proportion of seed sown determines the proportion of harvest.

> Remember this; whoever sows sparingly will also reap sparingly, and whoever sows generously will reap generously. (2 Corinthians 9:6)

8. Don't sow a seed at the expense of generosity, whether generosity to the things of God or to fellow human beings.

> You have planted much, but have harvested little. You eat, but never have enough. You drink, but never have you fill. You put on cloths, but are not warm. You earn wages, only to put them in a purse with holes in it. (Haggai 1:6)

Don't let your expenses and investment plans disturb or delay you from doing good deeds.

9. Seed-sowing is painful, but reaping is gainful.

> Those who sow in tears
> Will reap with songs of joy. (Psalm 126:5)

Truly, sowing is very painful, but reaping is very gainful. Sow in tears today that you may reap in joy tomorrow! There is no other way to abundance other than continuous sowing. If you sow little, it is very certain that you will not reap more than what you have sown. Indeed, God's principle of abundance is hidden in the principle of sowing.

TYPES OF SEED PEOPLE SOW

1. Natural Seed

This is a kind of agricultural works or farming which enables the world to have food security. Except in a rare situation, sowing natural seed always brings bountiful harvest. A grain of maize or corn can yield over 1,000 of its kind. An example of a person who sowed natural seed in the Bible is Isaac.

2. Spiritual Seed

We have seen people that sacrificed their lives for courses they believed in and brought fame and fortune. Martin Luther, the great reformer of the church, risked his life to bring transformation to global church in the sixteenth century. Mother Teresa in India risked her life to care for the sickly and the needy. Nelson Mandela, the late former president of South Africa, risked his life and spent twenty-seven years behind bars to fight against social injustice in his country. Martin Luther King laid down his life to fight against racism and white domination in USA; even though he lost his life, the world has not stopped paying homage to him, and President Barrack Obama is a beneficiary of the seed sown by him (Martin Luther King). However, Jesus Christ remains the greatest example of someone that sowed his life for the benefit of the entire human race.

3. Financial Seed

This can be done through investment and by being generous and charitable. The popular saying 'Nothing ventured, nothing gained' is sacrosanct when it comes to financial success. I read how that great financial and industrial wizard John D. Rockefeller of United States of America started his business empire with two dollars and fifty cents loaned to him by his biological father. His net worth today—even posthumously released three years ago—is said to be worth over 400 billion dollars.

Learn the secret of starting small and make sure you invest if you want a change of story in your finances.

> Do not be deceived: God cannot be mocked. A man reaps what he sows. (Galatians 6:7)

4. Seed of Good Work

Someone has said your success in life will not be measured by your consumption but rather by your contribution. Opportunity to do good to others no matter how small must not be overlooked or allowed to pass by. Dr Fleming, who invented penicillin, would have ended up being uneducated but for the generosity of a great parliamentarian statesman, Churchill. It is noteworthy that penicillin saved the life of Winston Churchill, the son of Churchill senior, from untimely death. Winston eventually became the prime minister of the United Kingdom during WWII and stopped the total collapse of world civilization. Can you see the multiple effects of a singular seed of good work done?

> In Joppa there was a disciple named Tabitha (which, when translated, is Dorcas), who was always doing good and helping the poor. (Acts of the Apostles 9:36)

Dorcas was a very good example of someone that sowed a seed of good works and whose good works spoke on her behalf.

5. Seed of Evil Work

An adage says, 'Whatever a man does lives after him.' The law of karma guarantees that whatever you sow you will reap. It is ironical that many people choose to sow evil seeds—hatred, confusion, oppression, crime, cheating, murder, disunity, and many more. After several years, their harvest will come either in their lifetime or after their demise.

An example of evil seed-sowing is by Adoni-Bezek, a king described in the Bible passage quoted below. He was an expert in capturing kings and cutting off their thumbs and big toes; at least seventy kings suffered this fate in his hands. When the Lord gave him to the hands of Israel, the same thing was done to him.

King Adoni-Bezek sowed evil seeds and reaped what he sowed, as seen in Judges 1:4–7. Remember, what you sow you shall reap.

A WAY TO ESCAPE

Even if you have been sowing evil seeds per adventure, there is an opportunity for you to make a U-turn, and one good thing about God is that he will forgive you and possibly prevent a harvest of nemesis.

If you are a child or a relative to someone who had sown evil seeds and you seem to be plagued by their evil legacies, you can claim your freedom by invoking the Word of God, as recorded in the Bible passage below;

'What do you people mean by quoting this proverb about the land of Israel: "The parents eat sour grapes, and the children's teeth are set on edge"? As surely as I live, declares the Sovereign Lord, you will no longer quote this proverb in Israel. For everyone belongs to me, the parent as well as the child—both alike belong to me. The one who sins is the one who will die.' (Ezekiel 18:2–4)

If you want your story to change, go and learn the principle of sowing seeds often and deliberately. Even if the harvest is delayed, keep on sowing; sooner than later, you will reap bountifully.

Don't eat your seed! Learn to sow when it is easy and when it is not.

CHAPTER 6

THE PLACE OF FORGIVENESS IN A CHANGE OF STORY

Then Peter came to Jesus and asked, 'Lord, how many times shall I forgive my brother when he sins against me? Up to seven times?' Jesus answered, 'I tell you, not seven times, but seventy times seven times. Therefore, the kingdom of heaven is like a king who wanted to settle accounts with his servants. As he began the settlement, a man who owed him ten thousand talents was brought to him. Since he was not able to pay, the master ordered that he and his wife and his children and all that he had be sold to repay the debt. The servant fell on his knees before him. . . . "You wicked servant," he said, "I cancelled all that debt of yours because you begged me to. Shouldn't you have had mercy on your fellow servant just as I had on you?" In anger his master turned him over to the jailers to be tortured, until he should pay back all he owed. This is how my heavenly father will treat each of you unless you forgive your brother from your heart.'

Matthew 18:21–35

This passage presents to us a great teaching on one of the most sensitive and nerve-touching issues in the world today. This deals with offense and forgiveness. There is no way we can live as human beings without offending people and being offended. Some offences are mild, while some are grievous, yet we must find a way to deal with this serious issue.

While it is relatively easy for few people to easily forgive, many find it difficult, both Christians and non-Christians.

The apostle Peter went to Jesus and asked him how many times would his brother offend him and how many times would he have to forgive him. Then without waiting for Jesus' answer, he proposed seven times, but Jesus said that, rather, it was seventy times seven. The import of Jesus' formula here is on limitless forgiveness as it is practically impossible to be counting someone's offence until it reaches 490 times. Therefore, as you want people to forgive you when you offend them, you must extend the same generosity to people that offend you.

Siblings, friends, couples, trading partners, organizations, and nations will offend one another.

A story of a woman readily comes to my mind as I witnessed it in 1987 in a prayer meeting. The woman's only son who was a graduate fell sick. After all medical efforts failed, the mother brought her son to church for prayers. In the process of praying, it was revealed that animosity was existing between the woman and her husband. The man of God told the woman to go and reconcile with the husband if she wants her son to be healed, but the woman refused and opted for seven days of marathon fasting. Lo and behold, the son died shortly after she finished the marathon prayers, and she lost her hope and treasure because of the spirit of unforgiveness. If you want God to forgive you your sins, you must learn to forgive people.

The two strongest allied nations in the world today are United Kingdom and United States of America; this is possible because of forgiveness and forgetting the past as both nations have engaged in wars before, especially during the colonization of USA by UK.

One of the good legacies left behind by Nelson Mandela, late president of South Africa, and Olusegun Obasanjo, former president of Nigeria, is the establishment of the Truth and Reconciliation Commission, which is geared towards national healing, forgiveness, and reconciliation.

If as a nation this is being done, there is no reason why a similar thing cannot be done in feuding families, churches, friendship, etc.

Beloved, permit me to warn you that the miracle you have long awaited may elude you if you turn a deaf ear to the message contained in this chapter. In fact, it may be difficult for you to make it to heaven as the Bible says that the foundation of God stands sure.

The Bible verses quoted above tells us about a wicked servant who embezzled his master's thousands of talents; when the master found out and wanted to cast him into prison, the servant fell on his knees and pleaded for mercy. The master took pity on him, wrote off his debt, and forgave him.

This forgiven servant was on his way home when he saw a fellow servant who owed him 100 denarii. He held the fellow servant by the throat and was determined to choke him to death. Turning a deaf ear to all entreaties to spare the debtor, he went ahead and ordered that his fellow servant be put into prison.

When the other servants heard, they were displeased and so reported the incident to their master, who became very angry with him. The master then sent for the wicked servant, ordered that he should be tortured and cast into prison.

To you, my beloved, reading this message is a wonderful opportunity for you to re-examine yourself. That torture you are going through in the hands of devils, witches, wizards, and others may have been permitted by God because of your unforgiving spirit. You are operating under closed heavens, and your prayers and fasting have no meaning to God because you have refused to show mercy to your fellow human beings, as established in the Bible:

> Then Joseph said to his brothers, 'Come close to me.' When they had done so, he said, 'I am your brother Joseph, the one you sold into Egypt! And now, do not be distressed and do not be angry with yourselves for selling me here: because it was to save lives that God sent me ahead of you. For two years now there has been famine in the land, and for the next five years there will not be plowing and reaping. But God sent me ahead of you to preserve for you a remnant on earth and to save your lives by a great deliverance. So then, it was not you who sent me here but God. He made me father to Pharaoh, lord of his entire household and ruler of all Egypt.' (Genesis 45:4–8)

> When Joseph's brothers saw their father was dead, they said, 'What if Joseph holds a grudge against us and pays us back for all the wrongs we did to him?'

So they sent word to Joseph, saying, 'Your father left these instructions before he died. This is what you are to say to Joseph: I ask you to forgive your brothers the sins and the wrong they committed in treating you so badly. Now please forgive the sins of the servants of the God of your father.' When their message came to him, Joseph wept. His brothers then came and threw themselves down before him. We are your slaves they said. But Joseph said to them, 'Don't be afraid. Am I in the place of God?' (Genesis 50:15–19)

According to the principle of human relations, there is every possibility for friction as we cohabit. No two human beings can live together and not offend each other from time to time. Neighbours will offend one another, co-workers of the same company or organization can have disagreements, and even members of the body of Christ may be at daggers drawn from time to time. But what matter most is to avoid harbouring bitterness in your heart because you can never receive grace and mercy from God if you do. But when we forgive one another from the bottom of our hearts, it is very certain that we ourselves will receive mercy from the throne of grace.

You may be a rich man, you may be a worker in the vineyard of the Lord, you may be a pastor or even a bishop, but you will miss heaven if you allow bitterness to take root in your heart, regardless of the anointing you carry. Bitterness is like a cancer; it festers until it consumes.

Genesis 45:4–8, quoted above, gives us an epic illustration of forgiveness. Joseph forgave his brethren from the bottom of his heart despite all they did to him.

In Genesis 50:15–19, Joseph's brothers had to lie to him, hoping he would be harsh on them since their father was no more. But thank God for his life, he still embraced his brothers.

There are many Christians today who have placed themselves in the position of God, but Joseph was humble, and that was why he said to his brothers, 'Am I in the place of God?'

What has happened to you may be part of God's intricate plans to take you to where you are today. Joseph would not have become a king in a foreign land if his brothers had not conspired against him and sold him into slavery in Egypt.

There is always a blessing in every disappointment, or better still, every disappointment is a blessing in disguise. In every situation you find yourself, there is always a lesson to be learned.

Beloved, my piece of advice to you is that you should learn to forgive your fellow brethren if you want your story to change. Remember that to err is human, but to forgive is divine.

WHAT IS FORGIVENESS?

Forgiveness can simply be defined as 'the act of writing off someone's offence, errors, or mistake whether the person apologizes or not'.

REASONS FOR FORGIVENESS

1. People offend one another.
2. We offend God and other people from time to time.
3. God forgave you, so you need to forgive others.

CONNECTION BETWEEN FORGIVENESS AND ANSWERED PRAYERS

> Therefore I tell you, whatever you ask for in prayer, believe that you have received it, and it will be yours. And when you stand praying, if you hold anything against anyone, forgive him, so that your father in heaven may forgive you your sins. (Mark 11:24–25)

In the quotation above, the Lord Jesus Christ was explaining to his disciples the need for forgiveness.

POWER OF FORGIVENESS

1. Forgiveness helps you to be healthy.

   > Some men brought to Him a paralytic, lying on a mat. When Jesus saw their faith, he said to the paralytic, take heart, son; your sins are forgiven. (Matthew 9:2)

2. It positions you for divine favour (Matthew 18:23).
3. It brings quick answers to your prayers (Mark 11:25).
4. Forgiveness gives victory over evil (Romans 12:7).
5. It gives grace to walk in the light of God.

   > But whoever hates his brother is in darkness and walks around in darkness he does not know where he is going, because the darkness has blinded him. (1 John 2:11)

Darkness, according to 1 John 2:11, means hating your fellow brethren. Many are living in darkness in the sight of God because of their unforgiving spirit. It is no wonder that God doesn't communicate with them any more.

Who is that person that has offended you?

What is their offence? And how grievous is it?

I beg you, in the name of the Lord, to let go. Remember, until you do, God may not show you mercy. May the Almighty God bless you and help you to let go of all forms of bitterness today in Jesus' mighty name!

CHAPTER 7

DIVINE ENCOUNTER FOR A CHANGE OF STORY

> As he went along he saw a man blind from birth.
> His disciples asked him, 'Rabbi, who sinned, this
> man or his parents that he was born blind?' . . . So
> the man went and washed, and came home seeing.
> His neighbors and those who had formerly seen him
> begging asked, 'Isn't this the same man who used to
> sit and beg?' (John 9:1–8)

This passage presents to us the story of a man that was born blind. It's worthy to take note that people, especially the Israelites, do not like to associate with the blinds, the lames, and people with other deformities (2 Samuel 5:6–8). They consider this set of people accursed or sinners that God is angry with, and so any form of association with them is shunned like plague. This was the situation of this man and his parents, and they continued to live with this stigma for several years until he became an adult and was confined to be a beggarly living. But one day, he had an encounter with Jesus that made him famous, and he became a controversial figure. This sudden change in his situation was so apparent and undeniable that people began to doubt whether he was the same person that they had known as a beggar or not.

I will never forget the story of a couple in my church several years back. They were barren, jobless, and living in lack. But despite their condition, they derived joy in serving the Lord. One day in 1995, the Lord sent me to them about the miracles He was about to do in their lives. I organized prayer sessions for them and began praying with them. Today, they have become parents of three lovely children. The husband got a job in an international organization, Ford Foundation, which offered free education and free medical treatment for four children besides the opportunity to travel abroad on holiday with his family members. They knew and always said the encounter with the anointing of God on my live was what brought such a wonderful transformation to their situation.

It may be possible that you have been going to church for a long time and had even gone to several crusades, revival, and prayer meetings without a change; I want to encourage you not to despair because the day of your encounter is surely here.

I have read through the Bible, and I have seen a commoner who became a person of worth, a slave being made a king, and a pauper who became prosperous.

Are you set for a change of story now? It is going to be from bad to good and from better to best. God will not change your story from good to bad.

The passage above gives us a brief story of a blind man who had a divine meeting with the Lord Jesus Christ, and there was controversy and argument because of his new status.

The story illustrates how today most of us are blind spiritually. Some move around aimlessly without a mission. Many lack direction because they are blind. It is only God that can direct anyone to the right path. Even the psalmist knew the importance and benefits of God's direction, and that was why he said:

> I will instruct you and teach you in the way you should go; I will counsel you and watch over you. Do not be like the horse or the mule, which have no understanding but must be controlled by bit and ride or they will not come to you. (Psalm 32:8, 9)

Most Christians today are living their lives like sheep without a shepherd, wandering about without direction. My dear reader, where are you heading to now? What is your mission at this moment?

When God told you to be a pastor, why did you choose to be an accountant? God is telling you to be a teacher, but why are you insisting on being a doctor? He sees ahead of you, and He knows what is good for you. Your eyes must be opened to see your future. You must regain your sight for a change of story. The late Pastor Myles Munroe said, 'Sight is the function of the eyes while vision is the function of the heart.'

Our problem is that when we are in one difficulty or the other, we attribute it to sin. The disciples wanted to know from Jesus if the blind man or his parents had committed any sin which had caused him to be born blind. But Jesus Christ answered that the man was born blind so that the power of God could be displayed in him.

Dr Bob Jones Sr said, 'Behind every glory there is a story.' What you are passing through now are stories that will beautify your glory in the nearest future. It is the story that makes glory shine.

The blind man had an encounter with Jesus Christ, and his life was never the same. I have seen God change many people's stories. The good Lord that changed the story of the blind man is very much alive, and I am sure if you have an encounter with Him, your life will never remain the same. All your rights that have been held up in the wrong hands shall be released unto you.

However, for you to have an encounter with the Lord, there are certain things you need to put into practice.

1. Obedience: Obedience takes a special and powerful place when it comes to having an encounter with the Lord. There are some whose stories have not changed because of disobedience. Disobedience to God's order, disobedience to God's teaching, disobedience to clear prophecy and dream. You are probably where you are today because you are full of disobedience. Disobedience can truncate your destiny. Be warned.
2. Sacrificial giving: This is also needed of you before having an encounter with the Lord.
3. Commitment to the work of God: Never say you are too busy when it comes to working in the house of God.

I am sure that if you abide by all these teachings, you will have a divine encounter with the Lord, which will consequently bring about the much-awaited change of story in your life.

CHAPTER 8

THE PLACE OF PLANNING IN A CHANGE OF STORY

O ne of the banes of problem we have in Africa is doing things haphazardly and awkwardly—no pun intended, just saying it the way it is and challenging us to change. The continent of Africa is facing enormous challenges today because our leaders, of yesteryears and today, failed and are failing to put a premium on proper planning—no family planning (many are giving birth to children they cannot train, nurture, and adequately feed), no financial plans (we earn and spend it anyhow), no town planning (most of our urban cities are experiencing flooding and traffic jam), and even no economic blueprints or plans for the emancipation of our populace. The scenario is micro-reflecting in many families and individual lives. Response to a simple question to an average person in Third World countries (like 'What would you like to do with your life?') will reveal the shallowness of the mind and shambled future of someone who intends to lead his country or organization tomorrow.

You *cannot* afford to live your life like this! The Bible, which is the Word of God, gives us the picture of God as a great planner. He carefully planned the works of Creation in details. The entire universe and galaxies reveal a creator that worked with plans. In many places and passages of the scriptures, we are exhorted to put our lives in proper plans.

Planning should cover all the gamut of your life—education, marriage, number of children to have, number of years working as an employee, where to live, when to retire, insurance purchases, spiritual life, going on vacation or holidays, and so many others.

There is a madness I noticed in south-western Nigeria, where I come from. People are good planners when it comes to ceremonies or events (marriage, naming, burial, house warming, etc.). Attention to details is always done on these social events, but the same people have no plans whatsoever—written or unwritten—about their lives. We cannot experience the change we crave for unless a clear departure from this type of lifestyle is made and a new foundation is laid for a life that is lived on deliberate planning.

> To man belong the plans of the heart, but from the Lord comes the reply of the tongue. (Proverbs 16:1)

> In his heart a man plans his course, but the Lord determines his steps. (Proverbs 16:9)

Many Christians are living their lives aimlessly. They wake up to go out without having specific goals for their lives. Many Christians don't even believe in planning; they believe it is the duty of our Heavenly Father to plan their lives. Yes, indeed, we have a father in heaven, but *He* has given us all that we need mentally to plan and live a well-organized life that will bring glory to Him.

The greatest evil that can befall any youth today is for him/her not to have a plan for his/her life. It irritates me when I see people, especially youths, who do not have plans and areas of focus for their future. They choose to forget that only few people have had their stories changed by chance. No amount of prayer and fasting can take the place of planning. If you don't begin to plan now, you may remain the same as you were years ago.

WHAT IS A PLAN?

A plan is a set of things to do to achieve a desired goal. These actions have to be what you are conscious of. It is true that many roads lead to greatness in life, but the main issue is, which way have you chosen to take? Do not wait for chance alone; learn to plan your life.

A plan is also a blueprint containing step-by-step actions aimed at achieving a predetermined purpose.

Who and what do you want to become in the next ten years? Do you know why many of us are failures? It is simply because we give up too soon on our goals. It is good to receive guidance and direction from prophets or counsellors, but you are the one who should set a goal for yourself. And how do you set goals? It is by planning your life.

A plan can also be referred to as a kind of design given by an architect to a potential landlord preparing to build a house.

> By wisdom a house is built and through under-standing it is established, through knowledge its room are filled with rare and beautiful treasures. (Proverbs 24:3–4)

Beloved, if you are waiting for luck, you will be locked up. This means that you will be stagnated. Don't ever depend on luck alone.

If you don't have detailed plans, you will not be able to build your house; you have to put the plan for your dream house in place. Likewise, your future needs concrete plans.

THE BENEFITS OF PLANNING

1. Planning helps you to set priorities to do the right thing at the right time. Should you become a graduate before getting married or otherwise? It will give you a set of priorities to follow in order to do the right thing at the right time.

2. Setting a plan for your life will allow for the effective utilization of your resources. What are resources? Resources may be money, education, talent, time, physical appearance, etc.

3. Planning will make it easy for the Holy Spirit to guide you. If you don't have a plan, the Holy Spirit cannot lead you. It was because the apostle Paul had the plan to preach the gospel in Europe that the Holy Spirit told him not to start from the east because there was danger there that may have terminated his ministry prematurely.

4. Planning brings success very close to your doorstep. If you know what you are to do and where you are going, you are already half successful. Our problems lie in our unwillingness or inability to plan.

5. Planning breaks a task into stages and makes evaluation easy. Once a plan has been made, it will

be easy to divide it into stages so that you will find out how well you are doing at the end of each stage.

THE METHODS OF PLANNING

1. Seek the face of God via prayer and fasting. To have a workable plan, do not be arbitrary, but rather, go to the one who made you in prayers. Ask him questions on His plans and intentions for your existence.

    > Now listen, you who say, 'Today or tomorrow we will go to this or that city, spend a year there, carry on business and make money.' Why, you do not even know what will happen tomorrow. What is your life? You are a mist that appears for a little while and then vanishes. Instead, you ought to say, 'If it is the Lord's will, we live and do this or that.' As it is, you boast and brag. All such boasting is evil. Anyone, then who knows the good he ought to do and doesn't do it, sins. (James 4:13–17)

    > There is no wisdom, no insight, no plan that can succeed against the Lord. (Proverbs 21:30)

2. Inculcate flexibility into your plans. No plan, no matter how good, is infallible or error-free. While it is bad not to have a plan, it is equally not good to be rigid in your plans. Room for adjustment, amendment, change of strategy should be factored in to any good plan. While your goal may remain

constant, the strategy to achieve it should be adjustable. Let your plans be flexible so that you can accommodate any adjustments or amendments.

3. Break your plan into short-, medium-, and long-term stages. Plans are said to be in three forms:

- Short term could be from one month to twelve months.
- Medium term could range from one year to three years or a maximum of five years.
- Long term is from five years and above. An example is a business meeting held by the board of Coca-Cola Company in the 1920s in USA which discussed ways on making everyone living on earth to have heard, known, or drank a bottle of Coke at the turn of the millennium.

4. Define your plans in concrete terms. Don't let your plan be vague or too loose-ended. Be specific. Make it measurable. Make it tangible. Make it achievable. Set deadlines for them. For example, you can give yourself a goal of becoming a PhD holder in seven years' time or have a goal of becoming a landlord in three years' time. Merely stating the goals is not enough; you must work out the nitty-gritty to bring them to reality.

Beloved, be informed that there is no luck anywhere. But luck only happens when preparation meets with opportunity. Go; learn how to plan. I pray the spirit of planning will be given unto you, and as you begin to plan, your story will change for good in Jesus' name. Don't forget that popular axiom: 'Failing to plan is planning to fail.'

As a concluding thought to this chapter, always bear in mind that proper planning prevents poor performance and failure to plan is planning to fail.

CHAPTER 9

THE PLACE OF GIVING IN A CHANGE OF STORY

The Lord appeared to Abraham near the great trees of Mamre while he was sitting at the entrance of his tent in the heat of the day. Abraham looked up and saw three men standing nearby. When he saw them, he hurried from the entrance of his tent to meet them and bowed low to the ground. He said, 'If I have found favor in your eyes, my Lord, do not pass your servant by. Let a little water be brought, and then you may all wash your feet and rest under this tree.' . . . He then brought some curds and milk and the calf that had been prepared, and set these before them. While they ate, he stood near them under a tree.

'Where is your wife Sarah?' They asked him. 'There, in the tent,' he said. Then one of them said, 'I will surely return to you about this time next year and Sarah your wife will have a son.' Now Sarah was listening at the entrance to the tent, which was behind him.

Genesis 18:1–10

Test always precedes testimony, and sacrifice always precedes success. The story of Father Abraham in the passage above gives us a clue to what can come our way sometimes before we get what we desire.

Abraham and his wife, Sarah, were old, well stricken in age, and childless. They had every reason to be aggressive, be unaccommodating, avoid everybody around them, and not to talk of entertaining unknown visitors. But one day, three men appeared before his tent, and Abraham promptly welcomed them, gave them water and cow's milk, and instructed his wife, Sarah, to prepare a delicious meal for them, while his servants were instructed to slaughter a tender calf for the visitors.

After the visitors have eaten and were satisfied, they asked for his wife and declared that, in a year's time, Sarah would become a mother of a male child. This sounded very unbelievable to the couple, considering their age. Sarah was 89 years, while Abraham was 99 years.

It was the act of giving and generosity that helped Abraham and Sarah not to miss their time of visitation. Since no one knows his time, a continuous act of generosity should be sustained and encouraged as you won't know whether the person you will help will lead to a change of story in your life. Your life is meaningless if it is not employed in the service to humanity. Your achievements are vanity if they are not targeted at helping others.

Be informed that God has given you to your generation as a gift. The Lord has given you to that place as a gift, and if you refuse to play your role, your story will not change. The first verse of the above quote says, 'The Lord appeared unto Abraham.' If you want unusual things from the Lord, you must begin to do unusual things.

Giving is a complex word that covers many areas in the gamut of life. God is the greatest giver. He is the giver of connection. He is the giver of peace. He is the giver of joy. He is the giver of knowledge. He is the giver of wisdom. He is the giver of breakthroughs. I tell you, He is the giver of all things, and He gave us the ultimate gift—His only begotten Son.

> For God so loved the world that He gave His one and only son, that whoever believes in him shall not perish but have eternal life. (John 3:16)

God is a great, prodigious, and wonderful giver. Thank God for the life of Father Abraham; he was a spirit-filled man. He was a generous man; otherwise, he would have missed out on that wonderful opportunity.

If you want your story to change, the logic behind it is very simple: just learn to give with your whole heart.

Mama Sarah would have died as a barren woman but for her submission and obedience to her husband's directive, which eventually led to a change of story in her life.

Do you know that giving can prolong your days? And the mystery behind giving is that until you release what you have, you cannot get more in addition to what you are holding.

> But just as you excel in everything—in faith, in speech, in knowledge, in complete earnestness and in your love for us—see that you also excel in the grace of giving. (2 Corinthians 8:7)

The above quotation tells us the story of a church in the Bible—the Corinthian church. They were excellent in all areas but lacked the spirit of giving, and that was why the apostle Paul had to write to them from the Roman prison on the need for them to become givers.

THE POWER OF GIVING

- Giving will endear you to people.
- Giving makes you a channel of blessing to others.
- Giving has the power to save your life from danger.
- Giving helps you to project and represent God to people around you.
- Giving confers favour on people—the givers.
- Giving makes you get help in time of need.
- Giving helps in answering prayers (an example is that of Cornelius in Acts 10:3–7).

> One day, Elisha went to Shunem. And a well-to-do woman was there, who urged him to stay for a meal. So whenever he came by, he stopped there to eat. She said to her husband, I know that this man who often comes our way is a holy man of God. . . . So he called her. You have gone to all this trouble for us. Now what can be done for you? Can we speak on your behalf to the king or the commander of the army? She replied: I have a home among my own people. What can be done for her? Elisha asked. Gehazi said, 'Well, she has no son and her husband is old.' (2 Kings 4:8–14)

This is the story of the Shunammite woman who was generous to everybody around her, even to the man of God, Elisha. It was her generosity that made her a mother in life.

She was generous like Abraham and Sarah. Sarah did not turn down the words of Abraham and neither did the Shunammite woman's husband turn down the words of his wife and they both had sons as blessing from God. Do not allow your spouse or friend to discourage you when it comes to giving.

> 'Why do you call me good?' Jesus answered. 'No one is good except God alone. You know the commandments. Do not murder, do not commit adultery, do not steal, do not give false testimony, do not defraud, Honor your father and mother.' 'Teacher,' he declared, 'all these I have kept since I was a boy.' Jesus looked at him and loved him. 'One thing you lack,' He said, 'go, sell everything you have and give to the poor, and you will have treasure in heaven. Then come, follow me.' (Mark 10:18–21)

This passage talks about a man who came to Jesus to enquire about what he could do to make it to heaven. He had three uncommon blessings—he was rich, he was a ruler, and he was a young man. He asked Jesus what he could do to inherit the kingdom of God. After much discussion, Jesus concluded that he lacked one thing and not until that thing was done would he be qualified to make it to heaven.

And what did the young man lack? He lacked the spirit of giving. This message is going to all of you beloved brethren out there. Unless you have the spirit of giving, your story cannot change in life, and you may not even make it to heaven.

I pray the spirit of giving shall be given unto you in Jesus' name. Amen!

CHAPTER 10

THE PLACE OF PRAYER IN A CHANGE OF STORY

I grew up to know my mother's best and intimate friend, Madam Omotoso Rachael Abiodun, whom I dubbed my second mother because of the closeness of both families. But she had a challenge immediately after her marriage. Her first four children died, and afterwards she couldn't conceive again. This challenge made her to start moving from one prayer meeting to another.

At a point in time, she was even introduced to a native doctor, popularly called *babalawo* (herbalist) in the Yoruba language. When she couldn't get a solution from this herbalist, who refused to give her anything as a panacea to her problem, she then decided to lock herself up in a room to seek the face of God in prayers, with the instruction to her husband never to open the door until the day she herself would knock.

After several days in prayers, on the fourth day, it was revealed to her in a dream that an evil mark the size of a coin was placed on her. She was told in her dream of the steps to take to get the evil mark removed. After obeying the directives she got from this prayer exercise, she became a proud mother of five good children, who are today doing very well.

> Jabez was more honorable than his brothers. His mother had named him Jabez, saying 'I gave birth to him in pain.' Jabez cried out to the God of Israel, 'Oh, that you would bless me and enlarge my territory! Let your hand be with me, and keep me from harm so that I will be free from pain.' And God granted his request. (1 Chronicles 4:9–10)

WHAT IS PRAYER?

Prayer is the art and science of communication between God and his subjects—human beings or creatures.

WHY IS PRAYER A SCIENCE AND AN ART?

Prayer is an art because it is something you have to learn. Prayer is a science because nobody knows how it works; there is a mystery behind it.

Everybody knows that prayer works. Everybody believes in prayers. Nobody has ever seen God physically yet, we talk and communicate with Him in prayers. We are talking with someone higher than we are, and we can choose to call Him different kinds of name. Some call Him Eledumare, some call Him Chukwu, some call Him Allah, while some call Him Osanobua. Yet He listens to all without prejudice based on tribe, religion, or ethnicity.

The above scriptural quotation contains a brief story of an unlucky man given birth to by an unlucky woman. The mother gave birth to him (Jabez) in pain and distress. But to the glory of God, he knew the power of prayers; he went back to his creator in prayers, and his story changed. The reason why many stories have not changed may be because they have missed the principles and practices of prayer.

ANALYSIS OF THE PRAYER OF JABEZ

1. 'Oh that you will bless me.' Jabez was living a poverty-ridden life. He was specific and prayed directly for blessing.
2. 'Enlarge my territory.' He was squatting even as an adult. That was why he told God to enlarge his territory.
3. 'Let your hand be with me.' He knew that when the hand of the Lord is upon someone, exaltation, success, freedom, exploits, and victory will be the result.
4. 'Keep me from harm.' Jabez knew that evil existed in the world, and he knew also that only God can provide protection from evil.
5. 'I will be free from pain.' Nothing is as painful as living in frustration and poverty. Nothing seems to work in his life. He became an object of mockery. But God heard his prayer, and his story changed. God granted his requests!

THE PRINCIPLES OF PRAYER

1. Position

You may sit down, lie down, close your eyes, or keep them open. You may even decide to be rolling on the ground or to stand up throughout the period of prayer. You may decide to be naked, but this should be done in private.

2. Procedure

Worship God.

> Enter his gate with thanksgiving; go into his courts with praise. Give thanks to Him and praise his name. (Psalm 100:4)

3. Rules and Regulations

Confess your sins and never keep malice. Let your heart be free so that the Lord can dwell in you.

THE EXPLOITS OF PRAYER (IN BRIEF)

1. Prayer Changes Stories

Hannah's and Jabez's stories changed after they prayed.

2. Prayer Moves Mountains.

The Red Sea was a mountain to the Israelites, but after prayers, the mountain was moved.

3. Prayer Quickens the Dead

A very good example of this is the story of Lazarus, who was brought back to life four days after his death.

4. Prayer Revitalizes Spiritual Life

Engage in constant prayer to keep your soul and spirit alive and connected to God.

5. Prayer Empowers

When you pray, you will be empowered and invincible that no power will be able to stand against you.

6. Prayer Unties the Chains of Enemies

Prayer breaks unseen and spiritual fetters.

> Around midnight, Paul and Silas were praying and singing hymns to God, and the other prisoners were listening to them. Suddenly, there was such a violent earthquake that the foundations of the prison were shaken. At once all the prison doors flew open, and everybody's chain came loose. (Acts of the Apostles 16:25–26)

7. Prayer Sets You Free from Bondage

What kind of bondage are you in? Rest assured that your life will never remain the same after prayers.

8. Prayer Opens Prison Doors

The release of Paul and Silas from jail was a clear example that prayers can open the most secured prison doors.

9. Prayer Compels Divine Intervention

In Acts 12:1–8, The apostle Peter was freed from prison.

10. Prayer Shuts the Mouths of Lions

Daniel's story readily comes to mind.

Now when Daniel learned that the decree had been published, he went home to his upstairs room where the windows opened towards Jerusalem. Three times a day he got down on his knees and prayed, giving thanks to his God, just as he had done before. Then these men went as a group and found Daniel praying and asking God for help. So they went to the king and spoke to him about his royal decree. Did you not publish a decree that during the next thirty days anyone who prays to any god or man except to you, o king would be thrown into the lions' den?

The king answered, the decree stands—in accordance with the laws of the Medes and Persians, which cannot be replaced. Then they said to the king, Daniel, who is one of the exiles from Judah, pays no attention to you o king . . . my God sent his angel, and he shut the mouth of the lions. They have not hurt me, because I was found innocent in his sight. Nor have I ever done any wrong before you o king. (Daniel 6:10–22)

The lion you are facing today may not be physical like that of Daniel, but I believe that with prayers, the mouth of that lion will be shut.

11. Prayer Brings Transformation

The power and potency of prayer to bring about a change of story is indescribable and incomprehensible.

I am a living testimony to the transformative power of prayers. The years 1987 to 1990 were what I usually refer to as a dark period in my life. But graciously, it also doubled as a period I was trained in the art and act of prayer. Today, God has transformed my life so much that it is difficult to believe what I went through during that period. Till today I still receive answers to some of the prayers I said then—twenty-eight years after.

12. Prayer Reduces Anxiety

Anxiety is one of the social and psychological problems bedevilling many today. But it has been proved that people who engage in constant prayer worry less, while those who do not pray are chronic worriers with attendant evils, like depression, sorrow, hypertension, and insomnia.

13. Prayer Opens the Door of Opportunity

Are you a jobseeker? Are you an admission-seeker? Or you are trusting God for a good spouse? I encourage going to the place of prayer. Prayer removes barriers, obstacles, and stumbling blocks, and it renders opposition forces powerless.

> Devote yourselves to prayer, being watchful and thankful. And pray for us too that God may open a door for our message, so that we may proclaim the mystery of Christ, for which I am in chains. (Colossians 4:2–3)

Go and practise prayer. Go and devote yourself to praying. Go to your closet and pour your heart to God in prayers. He is always ready to hear and answer you. Henceforth, you will no longer experience evil and sorrow in your life, and the good Lord will enlarge your coast for a change of story. Amen.

CHAPTER 11

THE PLACE OF PRAISE IN A CHANGE OF STORY

The Bible in one of its epic stories introduced us to the power inherent in praise. The tiny nation of Judah was confronted with a battle against three allied greater nations—Moabites, Ammonites, and Mount Seir (Edomites). The intention was to devastate Judah and totally destroy it. King Jehoshaphat, being a godly king, proclaimed fasting and prayers for all and sundry in Judah. In the process of praying, a prophecy came out, assuring Judah of victory over these enemy nations but with the instruction not to engage in physical battle but in praises.

The following day, in obedience to this revelation, choir services were engaged with trumpeters, timbrels, and other musical instrumentalists and singers marching towards the battle line. Surprisingly, on getting to the battleground, all the soldiers of the enemy nations were dead, and they started to take the spoils of war, which lasted three days.

You can read this exciting and inspiring story on the power of praise in 2 Chronicles 20:1–30.

May God be gracious to us and bless us and make his face shine upon us, that your ways may be known on earth, your salvation among all nation. May the peoples praise you, O God; may all the peoples praise you. May the nations be glad and sing for joy, for you rule the peoples justly and guide the nations of the earth. May the people praise you, o God
May all the peoples praise you.
Then the land will yield its harvest
And God, our God, will bless us
God will bless us,
And all the ends of the earth will fear him. (Psalm 67:1–7)

The psalm quoted above was written in 537 BC in Babylon by an unknown author. The background story of this psalm can be seen in Daniel 9:1–19.

It is interesting that a psalm of praise of this type was written in the land of captivity when it was expected that people would be mourning or weeping. This shows that the writer understood the power of praises.

SYNONYMS OF *PRAISE*

- *thanksgiving*
- *appreciation*
- *gratitude.*

Great people have discovered and employed the weapon of praise and gratitude to achieve their life's goals. People who lived without knowing this secret lived a miserable life.

If you want to be happy, be thankful.

If you want increase, be praiseful.

If you want quick answers to prayers, show gratitude to God on the things you already have.

Praise and gratitude are better expressed through songs and words of commendation. Even if an employer learns to praise his/her employees, he/she would get the better part of them. Conversely, an employee will get a pay raise and promotion faster if he/she learns to show gratitude to his employer instead of going about murmuring and complaining. If the foregoing is true about human beings, how much more with our Creator?

Beloved, if you want your story to change, go and learn how to use the weapon of praise. I urge you to do away with murmuring and grumbling. Do you know why you are still in that problem? It may be due to the fact that you have not learned how to use the weapon of praise.

Do you know that when you pray, God sends down His angels from heaven and when you praise God, He will leave His throne to come down? I tell you the truth; God dwells in the praises of His people. Your story may not have changed because you have not learned how to pray with praise.

The writer of Psalm 67 further revealed that, after the people had offered praises to God, the earth would yield its increase. Beloved, there is blessing in praising God. Your comatose business will yield its increase if only you learn how to praise God. Your house will yield its increase if you learn how to praise God concerning it. Your wife or your husband will yield their increase if you begin to praise God concerning them as from this present moment. That delinquent child that you have given up on will be saved if you continue giving praise concerning him to the Almighty God.

If you want success, if you want promotion, if you want wealth, if you want blessings, if you want breakthroughs that will forever keep the mouth of your enemies shut, go and learn how to praise God. Never forget that long life is certain if you learn to praise Him.

In my interactions with people in life I am always saddened that majority of them have only learned to share their trials and not their testimonies. If the constant complaints of these people affect me negatively, is it not possible that it makes the Creator feel unappreciated? Learn to praise God in whatever situation you find yourself!

How would you feel about a child who always grumbles despite your best efforts to satisfy him? So also will God not be happy if you are not a child that appreciates Him.

Beloved, if you want God's blessing, if you want your story to change, go and learn how to praise God.

Chapter 12

DIVINE ESTABLISHMENT FOR A CHANGE OF STORY

Being established is to be firmly rooted, grounded, and impactful with the attendant benefits that span generations. It is never the will of God that we should come to the world, live in it, and exit from it without making indelible marks. One of the compensations to the reality of death, which means leaving this world, is to be sure your memory lives on even when you are long dead. But there are forces—human, natural, environmental, and spiritual— that do not want this to be so.

Some years ago, a group of researchers carried out a research on why organizations/companies died. After a series of studies, they came up with four aggregate factors that usually led to the death of those companies.

- Paucity of funds: It was discovered that poverty and lack of funds or inadequate funding is one of the forces that kill companies. This is to say that money plays an important role in living an impactful life.

- Mismanagement of resources: This has to do with the lack of managerial competency. Achieving greatness or lasting value demands harnessing resources at your disposal to achieve a predetermined objective or goal. Resources here include money, materials, tangible and intangible assets, and personnel. Of all these resources, personnel is the most valuable and the most difficult to handle. Yet you must learn the rudiments of good people management to leave a lasting legacy.

- Unfaithful and corrupt staff: We are all witnesses to the death of several companies that were once vibrant and flourishing. At the back of this is mostly due to the activities of unscrupulous, unfaithful, and corrupt staff. The demise of a popular corporation in USA—Enron Corporation—attests to this point. If you want to be established trans-generationally, you need faithful people in your life.

- Untimely death of the visionary: This is the fourth factor identified as a cause of death of companies. Even though there is a popular axiom that says, 'Nothing succeeds like a successor,' it is important for a business concern or any organization to be nurtured to a level by the visionary before he/she dies. We have carcasses and wreckages of visions and institutions in our societies today that resulted from the untimely death of their promoters.

> May the favor of the Lord our God rest upon us;
> Establish the work of our hands upon us
> Yes establish the work of our hands. (Psalm 90:17)

This psalm was written by the prophet Moses in the year 1489 BC in the plain of Moab or Kadesh Barnea at the border of the Promised Land (Canaan land). Moses had the mandate of leading the children of Israel out of bondage in Egypt to the Promised Land. It was recorded that 600,000 men, excluding women and children, exited from Egypt.

> The Israelites journeyed from Rameses to Succoth. There were about six hundred thousand men on foot, besides women and children. (Exodus 12:37)

But as at the time he wrote this psalm, fewer than ten people were left; others have died in the wilderness within the spate of forty years without reaching their dreamed land. The errors these people made—rebellion against God, murmuring, ingratitude, backsliding, longing for the lives they once had in Egypt, unbelief, fear, and inferiority complex (grasshopper mentality)—led to their death in the wilderness without reaching their goals.

> We saw the Nephilim there (the descendants of Anak come from the Nephilim). We seemed like grasshoppers in our eyes, and we looked the same to them. (Numbers 13:33)

Moses, being their leader, had high expectations for these people and thought of great things they could do together when they got to the Promised Land, but he saw that all those dreams seemed unrealistic again. It was on this occasion that Moses penned down Psalm 90. He was prophetically pleading to God to spare his people, grant them his favour, and establish the works of their hands.

I have come to notice that when people are growing up, they have lofty dreams and visions of what they want their lives to look like, but as time wears on, these dreams become faded, forgotten, and sometimes unrealizable. This consequently leads to despair, depression, frustration, and outright failure.

I pray that your case will be different. You will not die in the wilderness of life, you will achieve your dream, and God shall establish the works of your hand in Jesus' name.

WHAT IS ESTABLISHMENT?

Many professionals have given different meanings to the word *establishment*, but taken literarily, it means 'to be firmly grounded'.

> Lord, you have been our dwelling place
> Throughout all generations
> Before the mountains were born,
> Or you brought forth the earth and the world
> From everlasting to everlasting you are God. (Psalm 90:1–2)

The truth is, if God doesn't establish the work of your hand, you will still end up being a failure, no matter the amount of money you have or the connections you can boast of.

AREAS TO FOCUS ON ESTABLISHMENT SUPPLICATION

1. Financial Establishment

Without being established financially, you are a failure. Getting established financially will position you to achieve all your goals in life. As the Bible says, 'Money answereth all things.' Without financial establishment, God's covenant on your life will be sabotaged irrespective of God's anointing on your life. Until you are established financially, you are not a prosperous Christian. You need this establishment so as to convince your family members and unbelieving neighbours that God is real. If you are in poverty, you are a disgrace to other Christians and God. The grace to be established financially shall be bestowed upon you in Jesus' name.

> But remember the Lord your God, for it is he who gives you the ability to produce wealth, and so confirms his covenant which he swore to your ancestors, as it is today. (Deuteronomy 8:18)

2. Establishment Beyond the Terror and Threat of the Enemies

I have discovered that fear is one of our major problems in Christendom—the fear of the unknown. Someone gave a suitable meaning to *fear* sometime ago:

F—fake
E—evidence
A—appearing
R—real

If you are truly a child of God, then you must be like your father. Your father is not a fearful person, so why should you live in fear? Who was that prophet that prophesied that you would not live to fulfil your days in life? Rise up and reject it in Jesus' name.

What brings fear?

- ignorance
- environmental happenings
- false visions
- bad dreams.

What are the causes of your fear?

- past failure
- death of loved ones
- threat of enemies
- negative experiences.

Beloved, I urge you to be rooted in the Lord: by so doing, you will have confidence in Him and live above terror and threats of your enemies.

> So do not throw away your confidence; it will be richly rewarded. (Hebrews 10:35)

3. Spiritual Establishment for Growth

The old axiom still holds true: 'A rolling stone never gathers mud.' There are many today that ought to be teachers but are still students in several churches. There are many that ought to be in leadership positions, but someone is still supervising them. They have refused to grow. And a child that refuses to grow is a child of sorrow.

In fact, though by this time you ought to be teachers, you need someone to teach you the elementary truths of God's word all over again. You need milk, not solid food! (Hebrews 5:12)

So then, just as you received Christ Jesus as your Lord, continue to live in Him, rooted and build up in Him, strengthened in the faith as you were taught, and overflowing with thankfulness see to it that no one takes you captive through hollow and deceptive philosophy, which depends on human tradition and the basic principle of the world rather than on Christ. (Colossians 2:6–8)

One of the major plans of God for you is to see you grow. So, child of God, what is preventing you from growing? But be informed that, before you can grow, you need to be spiritually established.

I am writing these things to you about those who are trying to lead you astray. As for you, the anointing you received from him remains in you, and you do not need anyone to teach you. But as His anointing teaches you about all things and as that anointing is real, not counterfeit just as it has taught you, remain in Him. (1 John 2:26–27)

Thank God for the Holy Spirit that was given to us to teach us all things. You need not be told before you pray; neither do you need anyone to tell you to read your Bible and fast. These are activities that can boost your spiritual life, and they ought to be a part of your life and living.

4. Career or Professional Establishment

There are failures today in all spheres of human endeavours. We all have those that are successful despite the situation of the global economy. No vacation, career, or profession is unimportant; neither does anyone thrust unearned success or greatness on anybody.

There's no job, career, or vocation that cannot make you rich and highly successful, but blessing and favour of the Lord are needed.

> The blessing of the Lord brings wealth, without painful toil for it. (Proverbs 10:22)

You won't be a mediocre in your profession; rather, you will be reckoned as one of the notable achievers in Jesus' name.

5. Marital Establishment

The rate at which married couples are separating and divorcing nowadays is alarming and frightening. No race, region, or religion is immune to this. Even clergy or gospel ministers are not spared!

This is not the will of God. Your own marriage can be an exception if you are ready to pay the price. Be patient with your spouse, and follow biblical teachings or principles on building a happy home.

> 'Haven't you read,' he replied, 'that at the beginning the Creator 'made them male and female,' and said, 'For this reason a man will leave his father and mother and be united to his wife, and the two will become one flesh' So they are no longer two, but one flesh. . . .

Jesus replied, 'Moses permitted you to divorce your wives because your hearts were hard. But it was not this way from the beginning. I tell you that anyone who divorces his wife, except for sexual immorality, and marries another woman commits adultery.'

The disciples said to him, 'If this is the situation between a husband and wife, it is better not to marry.' (Matthew 19:4–10)

Read also Ephesians 5:21–33. God can help you to navigate successfully the murky waters of the marriage institution. Don't give up yet on your partner. He/she can't be perfect or angelic since you are not perfect or angelic too.

May God keep your home from collapsing in Jesus' name.

I pray that you shall be established in all areas of your life in Jesus' name.

CHAPTER 13

CHALLENGES ALWAYS PRECEDE A CHANGE OF STORY

Stop looking for easy ways to greatness. Stop thinking about a road paved in gold to your dreamland. Stop believing you can achieve things of value without paying the price. Stop looking for shortcuts, and shun cutting corners. Nothing good and great comes easy.

Many tend to believe that when they are faced with tough situations or they encounter serious challenges, it is due to ill luck or bad luck. Reading through the stories of great men and women in life—yesteryears and today—reveals to us that they passed through tough times before getting to their destination in life.

Show me one person that you know that achieved something great and noble in life without a sizeable doze of struggle and pressure, and I will show you 1,001 people, both in the Bible and contemporary age, who achieved greatness despite lots and seasons of struggles.

Chief Obafemi Awolowo (the greatest president Nigeria never had—in the words of the late Odumegwu Ojukwu) became an orphan at a tender age of 8 without anyone to train him in school or to serve as foster parent. He was exposed to affliction and hardships so early in life and could not afford formal education beyond standard six or so. He got himself educated through correspondence courses to become a stenographer (typist) and even went ahead and became a lawyer—a renowned lawyer for that matter. He also became a premier in western region of Nigeria with a legacy that has not been surpassed by any other politician till date. The first television, radio station, stadium in Africa and the first twenty-five-storey building in Nigeria were recorded during his tenure as a premier.

History makes us know that, at a point in time, he took a bank loan using a house as collateral. The business went bad, and he lost the house to the bank, which was bought by another person. He continued to labour until he had a breakthrough and had enough money to repurchase the house. This man by all standards was a great politician, an astute manager of people and resources, a great lawyer, a great thinker, a great industrialist, a pan-Africanist, a great husband, a successful father, and a global icon.

All these were made possible because he never saw those early days' challenges as ill luck or problems to shy away from. Rather, he chose to confront them head-on, defeated those challenges, achieved greatness, and fulfilled his destiny.

You can do the same!

> There was a Benjamite, a man of standing, whose name was Kish son of Abiel, the son of Zeror, the son of Bekorath, the son of Aphiah of Benjamin. He had a son named Saul, an impressive young man without equal among the Israelites—a head taller than any of the others.

Now the donkeys belonging to Saul's father Kish were lost, and Kish said to his son Saul, take one of the servants with you and go and look for the donkeys. So he passed through the hill country of Ephraim and through the area around Shalisha, but they did not find them. They went on into the district of Shaalim, but the donkeys were not there. Then he passed through the territory of Benjamin but they did not find them. (1 Samuel 9:1–4)

WHAT IS A CHALLENGE?

A challenge is an unusual occurrence or something that stresses you and places a demand on you. It is another name given to a problematic situation.

A very critical assignment was given to Saul, a challenge to look for what was lost. His father sent him on this errand, and it was not possible for him to turn down his father's request.

Many of us today are seriously looking for the thing that is missing in our lives, and instead of us calling it a challenge (critical assignment), we see it as a problem.

DIFFERENT KINDS OF CHALLENGES

1. Disappointment by a fiancé or fiancée: A fiancé or a fiancée is someone you are engaged to and are planning to get married to. Being disappointed by your fiancé or fiancée is a situation you should

choose to perceive as a challenge and not a problem. You should have it at the back of your mind that every disappointment is a blessing in disguise. It is possible that the marriage may break up in the future if you eventually get married and that God has prepared a better person for you.

2. Threat of eviction from the place of abode: If you are being disturbed or threatened by landlords, don't harm yourself because of it. God shall make you a landlord soon.

3. Loss of a job: Don't see the job you lost as a family background problem. God is grooming you to become a managing director or an entrepreneur of your own company.

4. Sickness: Refrain from considering sickness as punishment. A person who has suffered physical pain and confinement is in a good position to do something to help others that are suffering as he/she once had. Your ministry may be in the making!

5. Threat of divorcement: The threat of divorcement has drawn many closer to God. It has turned many to prayer warriors. God may be using it to bring you closer to Himself.

6. Loss of loved ones: Examples may be the death of a child, husband, or wife. Some widows met with Christ in the Bible, and their lives were transformed forever. Maybe if they had not lost their husbands, they would not have found Christ.

7. Critical assignment: This assignment may lead to your promotion. Saul might have lost the chance to become a king if he had turned down his father's assignment. What kind of assignment has

been given to you? I urge you to go back to that assignment today and stop dodging responsibility.

8. Threats of enemies: Do not be afraid of the threats of enemies. All you need to do is to pray and trust in God. Encourage yourself with the story of David and Goliath.

9. Childlessness: This is another challenge that many people see as a big problem. The devil might intend to block your womb when you are about to encounter a change of story, but worry not. Always pray, fast, and put your trust in God. You will be the Hannah, Sarah, and Elizabeth of this generation.

10. Lack of food, money, water, and trusted friends etc. Scarcity and lack of basic things in life can be worrisome, but they also can spur you on to resourceful thinking that will lead to uncommon breakthroughs.

THE BENEFITS OF CHALLENGES

1. Challenges are forerunners to miracles, signs, wonders, blessings, and breakthroughs. Just as darkness is the forerunner to light, so is struggle the forerunner to success. A perfect example is the excruciating pain women undergo during labour before they become mothers.

2. They awaken our sense of seriousness.

3. Challenges prevent complacency. It makes a person work harder, shun laziness, and shun grumbling. It pushes students to study hard so as to be successful in their academics.

4. Challenges draw people closer to God.
5. Challenges give impetus to fasting and prayer.

Beloved, what are those things that are stressing you at the moment? Know that some challenges are what God uses to bring the best out of you. Never give up, don't go back to bed, and don't resign to fate yet. A miracle is waiting for you!

CHAPTER 14

THE PLACE OF MERCY IN A CHANGE OF STORY

In the year 2004, God taught me a great lesson on obtaining mercy by showing mercy. I was in my office around noon one day when a totally strange man entered our church compound and demanded to see me. He walked into my office and told me a pathetic story about his situation.

This man was an evangelist having a music ministry in Ondo, Ondo State of Nigeria. A member of his church loaned him money to wax his album, which he refunded, leaving him with a 10,000-naira balance. Upon his failure to pay this balance when due, he was arrested by policemen based on the petition written against him by his creditor. He came over to Lagos to meet his elder brother for financial assistance, but on arrival, he learned his elder brother was out of a job (he lost his job a month earlier). Someone who knew the philosophy of our church for helping the needy directed him to me.

At this particular time, our church worship auditorium was under construction, and we didn't even have enough money to pay for that day's labour wages. I sent for Pastor Oladipo Matthew (who was supervising the job) to enquire how much we had at hand. It was the exact sum the stranger was looking for, while that day's wage bill was over 20,000 naira. I decided to give the stranger the money and believed in God for a miraculous provision.

Not quite long after he left, someone that I had seen last for close to one year called me and demanded to see me (this man is not our church member). When he came, he brought a tithe of 132,000 naira to the church. Pastor Matthew, who had been reluctant to release the money to the stranger and asked how I would tell the labourers that there was no money after the day's job, was surprised about the positive turn of events. I resolved that day that nothing will ever stop me from showing mercy to people.

> I assure you that there were many widows in Israel in Elijah's time, when the sky was shut for three and a half years and there was severe famine throughout the land. Yet Elijah was not sent to any of them, but a widow in Zarephath in the region of Sidon. And there were many in Israel with leprosy in the time of Elisha the prophet, yet not one of them was cleansed—only Naaman the Syrian. (Luke 4:25–27)

WHAT IS MERCY?

Mercy is a token of goodness given to someone who does not deserve it (unmerited favour). *Grace* is a synonym of *mercy*. Mercy is for the unworthy; mercy is for the simple at heart.

My beloved in the Lord, prayer and wisdom are gifts that are powerful, but I have come to know that mercy is more powerful!

Jesus Christ was telling his disciples about mercy in the passage quoted above. The story he was telling them happened many years before his birth. It was true that there were many widows in Israel, but God sent Elijah to the widow of Zarephath, an unbeliever. The widow of Zarephath only found mercy in the sight of the Lord. Likewise, Naaman the leper—another unbeliever—found mercy in the sight of his creator.

> Not only that, but Rebecca's children had one and the same father, our father Isaac. Yet, before the twins were born or had done anything good or bad—in order that God's purpose in election might stand; not by works but by Him who calls—she was told, the older will serve the younger. Just as it is written, Jacob I loved, but Esau I hated. What then shall we say? Is God unjust? Not at all! For he said to Moses, I will have mercy on whom I have mercy, and I will show compassion on whom I have compassion. It does not, therefore depend on man's desire or efforts, but on God's mercy. For the scripture said to Pharaoh. I raised you up for this very purpose that I might display my power in you and that my name might be proclaimed in all the earth. (Romans 9:10–17)

The mercy of God was bestowed upon Jacob instead of Esau because the Lord had decided to show mercy to Jacob, and no one could question Him on that.

POWERS OF MERCY

1. Mercy Is More Powerful Than Law and Judgement

Most preaching of our preachers today seem not to be in concordance with Christ's teachings. Even many preachers, in their zeal to keep members away from sinning, have diluted the pure teachings of Jesus on grace with the observance of law as a condition to obtain mercy and right standing before God, but a careful analysis of the New Testament teachings of Christ will give a different picture. While Jesus did not condone sinning, he made it clear that we can only have a right standing with his father by pure grace, which is mercy in other words.

In Matthew 9:13, Jesus said he desired mercy and not sacrifice. Therefore, mercy is more powerful than law and judgement, as exemplified in the passage below.

> Because judgement without mercy will be shown to anyone who has not been merciful. Mercy triumphs over judgement. (James 2:13)

> The teachers of the law and the Pharisees brought in a woman caught in adultery. They made her stand before the group and said to Jesus, 'Teacher this woman was caught in the act of adultery. In the law Moses commanded us to stone such women. Now what do you say?' . . . At this, those who heard began to go away one at a time, the oldest ones first, until only Jesus was left, with the woman still standing here. Jesus straightened up and asked her, 'Woman, where are they? Has no one condemned you?' 'No one sir,' she said. 'Then neither do I

condemn you,' Jesus declared. 'Go now and sin no more.' (John 8:1–11)

The adulterous woman found mercy not because she wasn't a sinner but the Lord just showed her mercy.

2. Mercy Gives Divine Help

What labour cannot do for you in the kingdom, favour can do effortlessly. It is evident from practical experience and careful observation that the race is not to the swift nor battle to the strong but that time and chance happen to them all. Many who seem to be godly and sometimes prayerful may find it difficult to make a headway in life, while a seemingly nominal Christian or even non-Christian gets things done easily. This is, of course, not a support for idleness, both physically and spiritually, but I am saying mercy can give you what you do not labour for sometimes.

> But let us come boldly to the throne of our gracious God. There we will receive his mercy, and we will find grace to help us when we need it. (Hebrew 4:16)

3. Mercy Guarantees Blessings

> Then Jacob prayed, 'O God of my father Abraham, God of my father Isaac, LORD, you who said to me, "Go back to your country and your relatives, and I will make you prosper," I am unworthy of all the kindness and faithfulness you have shown your servant. I had only my staff when I crossed this Jordan, but now I have become two camps. Save

me, I pray, from the hand of my brother Esau, for I am afraid he will come and attack me, and also the mothers with their children.' (Genesis 32:9–11)

Jacob confessed personally that he was not worthy of the blessings and favour he received. Ordinarily, a cheater, liar, and what have you are not supposed to be blessed by God, but Jacob's case differed, and this can be traced to the sheer mercy he received as he left his house and father's land empty-handed but came back full of blessings.

I pray that the Lord, who is not a respecter of anybody, shall have mercy upon you. Where people have refused to show you mercy, God will show you mercy.

SYNONYMS OF *MERCY*

1. *grace*
2. *favour*
3. *compassion*
4. *unfailing love*
5. *kindness*.

THOSE WHOSE STORIES CHANGED THROUGH MERCY

1. Bartimaeus the blind: Bartimaeus believed his story could change, and that was why he called out to Jesus to have mercy on him (Matthew 20:30).
2. Naaman the leper: it was the mercy that Naaman received that made him to be cured by the prophet Elisha (Luke 4:27).

3. The Zarephath widow: this widow also received mercy during a severe famine in the time of the prophet Elijah (Luke 4:25–26).
4. The thief on the cross: Jesus showed mercy to one of the thieves on the cross (Luke 23:42–43).
5. The apostle Paul: he received God's mercy and was called out to preach the gospel among the Gentiles (Galatians 1:15–16).

Mercy will distinguish you and make you to tower higher than your mate in life in Jesus' mighty name.

What your prayer, fasting, and labour cannot do, the Almighty God will release it unto you by His mercy.

CHAPTER 15

THE PLACE OF HOLINESS IN A CHANGE OF STORY

I had a near-embarrassing experience about eight years ago. I was invited as a speaker in an annual convention by a very senior pastor in my former denomination, which has a tradition that forbids members from using jewelleries. After a wonderful ministration and eulogy from the people, another visiting but equally senior pastor called me in the presence of about seven people and asked me loudly, 'What is that on your wife's ear and neck, and is it proper for a pastor's wife to use them?'

But for the Holy Spirit, he would have appeared holier and most righteous than me. I immediately noticed that this same pastor condemning my wife for wearing jewelleries had on him a golden wristwatch. I promptly replied by saying, 'Sir, what is that on your wrist?' He replied, 'A wristwatch.' I then told him that there was no difference between what he was wearing and what my wife was wearing except for the difference of the body parts on which they were worn. He was miffed and flabbergasted by this 'affront and arrogance' and could not talk again.

Upon reflection on this incident, I have come to realise that many Christians today and even church leaders are hypocritical because they do the same thing for which they condemn others.

> How then can a man be righteous before God?
> How can one born of woman be pure? (Job 25:4)

Holiness is a word with broad and controversial meaning, and that is why many theologians and scholars give different meanings to it.

Some define *holiness* as 'Christ living through us'. This is a good meaning, but I believe that it is an advanced definition of *holiness*. Others define *holiness* as 'the act of living a life without sin'. I so much disagree with that definition because there is no man on earth that can live a sin-free life. That was why Job asked God this question some thousands of years ago:

> What is man, that he could be pure,
> Or one born of woman, that he could be righteous?
> (Job 15:14)

We are mortals, and it is not possible for us to be pure. Job asked God this question some 1,500 years before Christ (Job 28:4), and not till Christ came to the world was there an answer to that question.

> God made him who had no sin to be sin for us, so that in him we might become the righteousness of God. (2 Corinthians 5:21)

God made Jesus Christ, who knew no sin, to be a sin so that we may be imputed with His righteousness.

WHAT IS HOLINESS?

> But if we walk in the light, as he is in the light, we have fellowship with one another, and the blood of Jesus, His son, purifies us from all sin. (1 John 1:7)

A holy person is a Christian who keeps a short account with God. He washes himself in the blood of Jesus every day but is not necessarily someone who is 100 per cent sinless.

Beloved, is there any man on earth that can live without committing sin? How many are keeping the Ten Commandments? We have more than 300 laws in the Bible. How many of us know these laws, and how many obey them? I discovered that our major problem is that we categorize sins. My dear, *sin is sin.* We don't need to deceive ourselves; nobody can live a sin-free life. What matters most is for us to keep a short account with God and continue to pray for victory over sin.

> But if you show favoritism, you sin and are convicted by the law as lawbreakers. For who keeps the whole law and yet stumbles at just one point is guilty of breaking all of it. (James 2:9–10)

What is the purpose of God's law?

> So the law was put in charge to lead us to Christ that we might be justified by faith. (Galatians 3:24)

The law is a tutor, which can be referred to as a pedagogue. God gave us the law to show the intensity of our sins and how helpless we are to keep the law so that when the saviour comes, we would be ready to accept him.

> For it is we who are the circumcision, we who worship by spirit of God, who glory in Christ Jesus, and who put no confidence in the flesh—though I myself have reasons for such confidence in the flesh, I have more . . . What is more, I consider everything a loss compared to the surpassing greatness of knowing Christ Jesus my Lord, for whose sake I have all things. I consider them rubbish that I may gain Christ.
> (Philippians 3:3–8)

The apostle Paul was trying to explain to the Philippians in the quoted text that he couldn't gain Christ with all his circumcision and birthrights as a Jew. Your spiritual pride is nothing; it is not a ticket to your being holy. Holiness is allowing Christ to live in us.

STAGES OF HOLINESS

The Bible reveals to us three stages of holiness as Christians.

1. Positional holiness: we are declared holy by accepting Christ as our Lord and Saviour (1 Corinthians 1:2).
2. Progressive holiness: we are being sanctified and purged of indwelling sin daily through the application of the blood of Christ (1 Thessalonians 5:23).
3. Permanent holiness: this type of holiness cannot be achieved here on earth, not until we get to heaven, when the tendency to sin will no longer be there and we'll no longer be subjected to the torture of this corrupt environment (Revelation 21:1–5, 19:6–8).

Jesus answered the question that was asked by Papa Job some 1,500 years BC during his earthly ministry.

> Jesus answered, 'I am the way and the truth and the life. No one comes to the father except through me.' (John 14:6)

I am proud to say that Jesus Christ is the answer to Job's question.

HOW TO ATTAIN HOLY LIVING

While attaining perfection may not be attainable as long as we are in this world and in the flesh, God expects us as his children to live a holy life or strive for a holy living.

Below are some steps that can help you in achieving progressive holiness in your daily living.

1. Flee from All Appearances of Evil

The apostle Paul exhorted his spiritual son, Timothy, to flee from any form or appearance of evil. An example of appearance of evil can be a Christian who is fond of visiting a pub and claiming not to be a drunkard or a fornicator or can be someone else who claims to be a Christian but is seen in an occult temple or ROF (Reformed Ogboni Fraternity) meeting and yet claims not to be a cultist. The focus here is on being sensitive to your environment—where you go to play, eat, or whatever.

> Reject every kind of evil. (1 Thessalonians 5:22, NIV)

> Abstain from all appearance of evil. (1 Thessalonians 5:22, KJV)

2. Guard Your Heart

The Bible says:

> Guard your heart with all diligence for out of it springs the issues of life. (Proverbs 5:22)

Your heart here is in reference to your mind or soul because that is the seat of your will, intellect, emotion, thoughts, and all other actions.

Jesus Christ said in Matthew 15:17–20 that out of the heart proceeds evil thoughts, adultery, and all other vices. The right question here should be, how do I guard my heart?

How to guard your heart:

- by being careful of what you hear

'Consider carefully what you hear,' he continued. With the measure you use, it will be measured to you—and even more. (Mark 4:24)

- by being careful of what you think
- by being careful of books you read
- by watching the music you listen to
- by being careful of movies you watch.

This foregoing will help you in guarding your heart.

3. Think the Things of the Spirit Always

Finally, brothers and sisters, whatever is true, whatever is noble, whatever is right, whatever is pure, whatever is lovely, whatever is admirable—if anything is excellent or praiseworthy—think about such things. (Philippians 4:8)

Even though we are a tripartite being that has soul, spirit, and body, we tend to live more in the flesh than in the spirit, and setting our minds on spiritual things will help in mitigating the influence of the flesh.

So I say, walk by the Spirit, and you will not gratify the desires of the flesh. (Galatians 5:16)

Set your minds on things above, not on earthly things. (Colossians 3:2)

4. Study the Bible Always

To be able to attain a measure of holy living, we must be ardent readers of the Bible.

> How can a young person stay on the path of purity? By living according to your word. (Psalm 119:9)

> I have hidden your word in my heart that I might not sin against you. (Psalm 119:11)

With the quotation above, you will see the importance of studying the Word of God in attaining a holy living.

5. Choose a Role Model

Jesus is the best role model. There is no spiritual goal you set for yourself that someone, somewhere, and sometime have not attained. A careful look at the Word of God and your church or Christian community will help you to identify someone who has lived an exemplary life and considered to be near saint. But I want to recommend the best role model to you—that is, Jesus Christ.

Take your time to study the four Gospel records (Matthew, Mark, Luke, and John) in the New Testament for graphic details and descriptions of Jesus Christ.

6. Engage in Self-Evaluation

A life not evaluated or assessed is a life not in balance. The Bible urges us to examine ourselves whether we are in faith or not (2 Corinthians 13:5). Self-evaluation will help you to know where you stand per the time in your Christian race and daily walk with the Lord. Self-evaluation will also help you make necessary adjustments in your lifestyle and possibly drop some habits that are ungodly.

Evaluation can be done by yourself or having an accountability friend who will be free to evaluate your life and tell you his observations without fear or favour.

7. Know That Your Body Is the Temple of God

God, as you know, is a spirit being who doesn't live in any physical temple or house. All those church edifices are built for our own convenience; where God lives is in our hearts. If your heart is the temple of God, then you can't afford to defile it by carefree living.

> Do you not know that your bodies are temples of the Holy Spirit, who is in you, whom you have received from God? You are not your own; you were bought at a price. Therefore honor God with your bodies. (1 Corinthians 6:19–20)

8. Pray Always for the Power to Live a Holy Life

Many Christians naturally wish to live holy but no one should undermine the power of the flesh, corrupt environment in which we live, demonic attacks and Satan's clandestine (secret and subtle) move to push Christians to do or act against the will of God. So prayer comes in here to fortify us spiritually in order to resist the tempter and the temptations.

> Finally, be strong in the Lord and in his mighty power. Put on the full armor of God, so that you take your stand against the devil's schemes. For our struggle is not against flesh and blood, but against the rulers, against the authorities, against the powers of this dark world and against the spiritual

forces of evil in the heavenly realms. . . . With this in mind, be alert and always keep on praying for all the Lord's people. (Ephesians 6:10–18)

It was prayer and fasting, as recorded in Gospel (records of Jesus Christ's life) of Saint Matthew in Matthew 4:1–11, that helped Jesus to defeat the tempter, Satan, and temptations. The same weapons will help you.

CHAPTER 16

THE INFLUENCE OF A GODLY FRIEND IN A CHANGE OF STORY

One of the greatest socio-relational blessings from God is the gift of friends. Right from childhood, people effortlessly enter into this filial relationship. The bond of friendship has been found to be very strong, sometimes stronger than the bond between siblings.

A friend is someone you relate to with a totally open heart. Someone said a friend is someone you can be with and speak with without censoring your thoughts.

> One who has unreliable friends soon comes to ruin, but there is a friend who sticks closer than a brother. (Proverbs 18:24)

But like everything in life that has a double edge, so also is friendship; it has both good and bad sides. Having a godly friend reduces your exposure to the risks that go with friendship. You must carefully and prayerfully choose your friends. While you are still a child or relatively young, this may be difficult, but as you get along in years, you must

113

sieve and shift the crowd of your acquaintances in order to pick a godly friend or friends.

> After David had finished talking with Saul, Jonathan became one in spirit with David, and he loved him as himself. From that day Saul kept David with him and did not let him return home to his family. And Jonathan made a covenant with David because he loved him as himself. Jonathan took off the robe he was wearing and gave it to David, along with his tunic, and even his sword, his bow and his belt. (1 Samuel 18:1–4)

The above biblical passage describes in graphic detail the story of two friends—Jonathan, son of Saul, and David, son of Jesse—who was in rivalry over the kingship title of Israel after King Saul, Jonathan's father.

Ordinarily and naturally, Jonathan should have conspired against his father to terminate his life and eliminate David. But because of the strong bond of friendship between them, Jonathan did not. The Bible says that the soul of Jonathan was knit to the soul of David, and Jonathan loved him as his own soul. Every Bible reader who is familiar with this story knows that Jonathan paid the supreme price by laying down his life for David.

The other friendship story in the Bible that superseded the story of Jonathan and David is that of Jesus Christ and his apostles.

> Greater love has no one than this: to lay down one's life for one's friends. You are my friends if you do what I command. I no longer call you servants,

because a servant does not know his master's business. Instead, I have called you friends, for everything that I learned from my father I have made known to you. (John 15:13–15)

WHAT IS FRIENDSHIP?

Friendship is a social relationship you enter into consciously or unconsciously. Friendship is one of the things we cannot avoid in the world, be it voluntary or involuntarily; it is very natural to discover that you are already in it. But you must bear in mind that friendship can lead to an untimely death, regret, failure as well as to happiness or success.

> When Job's three friends, Eliphaz the Temanite, Bildad the Shuhite, and Zophar the Naamathite, heard about all the troubles that had come upon him, they set out from their homes and met together by agreement to go and sympathize with him and comfort him.
> When they saw him from a distance, they could hardly recognize him, they began to weep aloud, and they tore their robes and sprinkled dust on their heads.
> Then they sat on the ground with him for seven days and seven nights. No one said a word to him, because they saw how great his suffering was. (Job 2:11–13)

In verse 11 of the passage quoted above, friends came to Job with the intention of comforting him due to the losses he just experienced. What a wonderful blessing to see people around you in times of difficulty!

The succeeding verse tells us his friends found it very difficult to recognize him. But why were his friends unable to recognize Job? The tide that befell Job had taken a toll on him and changed him beyond recognition. The suffering that will make people not recognize you shall not befall you in Jesus' name. Amen.

SYNONYMS OF *FRIEND*

1. *acquaintance*
2. *companion*
3. *soulmate*
4. *pal*
5. *buddy.*

THE EVILS THAT COME WITH CHOOSING A WRONG FRIEND

1. implication (when you choose a wrong friend, you are close to a prison yard because they are bound to implicate you)
2. debt
3. death
4. mockery (some friends are tempted to mock you in times of trouble, and that was why the psalmist said he would have borne it if only it was his enemy, instead of evil friends, who mocked him)

> If an enemy were insulting me, I could endure it;
> if a foe were raising himself against me, I could
> hide from him. (Psalm 55:12)

5. bad habits, like incest and rape (if only Amnon had
    not made Jonadab his friend, he wouldn't have been
    involved in such a bad/dirty habit)

> In the course of time, Amnon son of David fell in
> love with Tamar, the beautiful sister of Absalom
> son of David. Amnon became frustrated to the
> point of illness on account of his sister Tamar,
> for she was a virgin, and it seemed impossible
> for him to do anything to her. . . . 'Go to bed
> and pretend to be ill,' Jonadab said, 'when your
> father comes to see you, say to him, I would
> like my sister to come and give me something
> to eat. Let her prepare the food in my sight so I
> may watch her and then eat from her hand.' (2
> Samuel 13:1–5)

6. wrong counsel
7. wounds (evil friends can inflict wounds on you;
    never forget that they can even bring about your
    untimely death)

> If someone asks him, 'What are these wounds
> on your body?' He will answer, the wounds I
> was given at the house of my friends. (Zechariah
> 13:6)

BENEFITS OF A GODLY FRIEND

1. intimacy: you can be closer to them than your siblings.
2. sharing of joy: your friend will be there for you to share in your joy, like on graduation, child-naming, housewarming, birthday celebrations, etc.
3. sharing of burdens: an example is that of Job's friends who came to share his burden with him in his time of trial and tragedy.

Having said all this, I still urge you to make Jesus Christ of Nazareth your best friend. He is the best of all friends, and with him, you are safe.

> You are my friends if you do what I command. (John 15:14)

WHY SHOULD YOU CHOOSE JESUS CHRIST AS YOUR BEST FRIEND?

1. Jesus will give you life, joy, power, and connection with the highest being. He will give you an automatic access to God. Jesus said, 'I have not called you servants but friends.' It is great to have Jesus as a friend. I am happy to have Him as a friend. Who is your own friend? The Bible says, 'Can two walk together, except they be agreed?' Amos 3:3
2. He will stand by you at all times. I am not insane by saying it is good to have problems because it is during problematic times that one will know his/

her true friends. Usually, people that have dined and wined with you will quickly desert you when you run into one problem or the other. But the good news is that Christ will never desert you.

3. Jesus can be trusted.

> Beware of your friends; do not trust your brothers. For every brother is a deceiver, and every friend is a slanderer. (Jeremiah 9:4)

> Do not trust a neighbour; put no confidence in a friend. (Micah 7:5)

Don't put your trust in any human being; trust and lean on Christ alone.

4. You can confide in Jesus. You can put your confidence in Jesus; He won't betray you, and neither will you be disappointed. He is a wonderful friend. He can bless you, and He will never fail you. He won't let you down.

Remember that it was a friend (Andrew) who introduced Peter to Jesus, and his story changed (John 1:40–42). Beloved, I pray you have a friend like Andrew but always have it at the back of your mind that *Jesus is the best of all friends.*

CHAPTER 17

THE PLACE OF TIME IN A CHANGE OF STORY

Waiting time always appears long and frustrating, especially when a specific time frame about the waiting is not known or given. When you see others making waves, succeeding, progressing, getting married, buying cars, building houses, and enjoying life, apprehension and the tendency to ask when your own time will come are rife. But it is important to know that everyone has his/her allotted time from God. The fact that your mates are ahead of you today and you seem not to be getting anywhere does not mean that your own success, breakthrough, and testimony will not come.

In fact, this waiting time is usually a blessing in disguise to prepare you for the greatness ahead, to train you about the complexity of life, and to enable you to know how to manage success when it eventually comes.

Take, for example, the story of the sojourn of the children of Israel in Egypt. For 430 years, they were subjected to untold hardship, torture, oppression, and even enslavement. This continued as if there would be no end until the day the Lord opened a book of remembrance for them and sent a deliverer in the person of the prophet Moses.

I wouldn't know what you are passing through at the moment or how long you have been in that situation, but be assured that the Lord has not forgotten you and have a right schedule for your life. That great preacher in America, the late Bob Jones Sr said, and I quote:

> Dare you pray and the answers seem delayed be sure your God will come and he will never come late.

And the Bible also says:

> Surely there is an end and the expectation of the righteous shall not be cut off. (Proverbs 23:18)

Be assured that there is an end to the affliction plaguing your life. Be assured there is an end to living lonely as a single; the time of your marriage is approaching. Be assured there is an end to your joblessness, lack, pains, sickness, and mockery from detractors. I see an end very soon to these things, and I see a new beginning. A time of celebration, jubilation, testimony, change of story, and when you become the cynosure of all eyes is very near.

The Bible says:

> He has made everything beautiful in its time. (Ecclesiastes 3:11)

When your time comes, it will not only be beautiful but so glorious and timely that you will know that you couldn't have gotten it better at any other time.

Sometime later, Jesus went up to Jerusalem for a feast of the Jews. Now there is in Jerusalem near the Sheep Gate a pool, which in Aramaic is called Bethesda and which is surrounded by five covered colonnades. . . .

Then Jesus said to him, Get up! Pick up your mat and walk. At once the man was cured, he picked up his mat and walked. The day on which was a Sabbath, and so the Jews said to the man who had been healed, it is the Sabbath, the law forbids you to carry your mat. But he replied, the man who made me well said to me, pick it up and walk.

(John 5:1–11)

The man whose story appears in the biblical passage above was said to be bedridden for thirty-eight years. All hope seemed lost—no help, no helper, no comforter, no healer. It appeared that was how he was going to live his life and die, but at a time he never expected any help and possibly have lost hope, Jesus Christ, the great healer and helper, showed up and changed his story.

Listen, I see God stepping into your situation very soon. I see a new day and a new dawn in the horizon for you. You will overcome that battle. Your tears will come to an end. Your trial will turn to testimony. Today's story of lack in your life will turn to a story of abundance. You will yet praise him. Just believe.

THE MEANING OF TIME

Time is the yardstick by which the passage of life—either in hours, days, or other form of reckoning—is measured.

THE DIVISIONS OF TIME

Time is in seven divisions:

1. seconds
2. minutes
3. hours
4. days
5. weeks
6. months
7. years.

The psalmist said, 'My times are in your hands, oh Lord.' He was referring to these seven divisions of time.

THE USEFULNESS OF TIME

1. It helps us count our days.
2. It helps us give and keep appointments.
3. Time helps in determining the rate of one's progress or success.
4. It controls the period of sowing and reaping.
5. Time is a resource.
6. Time can be invested.

7. It is the greatest enemy of man if not properly planned.
8. Time is divine.
9. Time is a leveller; everyone, rich or poor, has only twenty-four hours per day.
10. Time is a healer; it heals physical, mental, and emotional wounds.

TYPES OF TIME

1. Clock time: This is our conventional time. It is the twenty-four hours of the day.
2. Real time: This is the worth of your time in a day. This is your lifetime. How are you living your life? Always remember that there will be an account on how you use your time as you have every responsibility during your cycle of time.

TIPS TO HELP IN THE USAGE OF TIME

1. Time has an expiry date.
2. Daytime is the best time to study, while night-time is meant for rest.
3. Reduce everything that brings about time wastage. Examples include gossip, oversleeping, addiction to television, etc.

THE PLACE OF TIME IN THE DIVINE ECONOMY

God, though not bound by time, usually chooses to work with time. There is what we call a *divine economy* in the theological world. This is the control of God in His world, using his own calendar to determine what happens and what does not happen to a nation, institution, family, or individual in such a perfect way that it will be difficult to fault Him.

An example of this is world civilization and economic prosperity. Civilization began in Africa and, by extension, economic domination. It later went to Europe, then later shifted to North America for over forty years now, but today, economic prosperity and domination seem to have moved to Asia. China seems poised to overtake USA as the number-one economic powerhouse in another ten years to come (unless the unforeseen happens) because it is the turn and time of the Asian continent. This shows that:

1. God is a god of order. He works with time.
2. there is an appointed time for everything and everybody.

   In the past God overlooked such ignorance, but now he commands all people everywhere to repent. For he has set a day when he will judge the world with justice by the man he has appointed. He has given proof of this to all men by raising him from the dead. (Acts of the Apostles 17:30–31)

3. God controls time and the destinies of all.

4. no matter how long your suffering may be, it will come to an end one day; it has an expiry date.

> For his anger lasts a moment but his favor lasts a lifetime; weeping may remain for a night but rejoicing comes in the morning. (Psalm 30:5)

> Now the length of time the Israelite people lived in Egypt was 430 years. At the end of the 430 years, to the very day, all the Lord's divisions left Egypt. Because the Lord kept vigil that night to bring them out of Egypt, on this night all Israelites are to keep vigil to honor the Lord for the generations to come. (Exodus 12:40–42)

Good news: Enemies cannot keep you in perpetual bondage. Your deliverance is on the way. Your freedom is at hand.

Don't despair. Don't give up. Don't commit suicide. The Israelites were in the bondage of slavery in Egypt for 430 years, but at a point in time, their deliverance came.

> You will get out of poverty to prosperity.
> You will get out of sickness to sound health.
> You will get out of struggles to successes.
> You will get out of barrenness to fruitfulness.
> You will get out of servitude to freedom.
> You will get out of suffering to surplus.
> You will get out of weeping to singing.
> You will get out of mourning to dancing.
> You will get out of burden to blessings in abundance.
> You will get out of obscurity to popularity.
> You will cross from being a servant to being a leader.

IT IS ONLY A MATTER OF TIME!

Wait on the Lord. Wait for the Lord.

> I waited patiently for the Lord;
> He turned to me and heard my cry. (Psalm 40:1)

I prophesy that by this time next week, next month, next year, your story will change in Jesus' mighty name.

INDEX

ABOUT THE AUTHOR

Onaolapo Gabriel Olusola is trained in the field of Marketing and Sales Management before been called into the Ministry in 1990. He is a gifted teacher, highly sought for conference and seminar speaker, charismatic preacher of the Word of God with a charming prophetic ministry.

The mandate of his calling is FREEDOM. He is usually been called an Apostle of freedom.

Besides being the founding pastor/president of Christ The King Rescue Global Ministry, a fast growing church based in Ogun State, Nigeria with branches in and outside the country, he is also the CEO of Gabriel Onaolapo Ventures and Olasunkanmi Mining Company Limited with interests in publishing and book sales, mining, real estate and farming.

He has authored many books among which we have titles like: Humble Beginnings, Optimism, Abundance, Freedom from Limitation, Freedom from Failure, Motherhood et al.

He got married 19years ago to Florence Taiwo Adenike-a pastor and school proprietress and they blessed with four children-Winner and Miracle (male twins) and two girls, Freedom and Queen.

HOW TO CONTACT US

Christ the King Rescue Global Ministry
Rescue camp ground
119, Agbado – Akute Road
Fakile layout, Giwa, Oke – Aro
Ogun state
Nigeria

Website – www.ckreglom.org
Email – vorep2006@yahoo.com
goriem2012@gmail.com
Telephone Numbers – 08033270387;
08056110022; 08034630505